THE MASTER TUTOR

A GUIDEBOOK FOR
MORE EFFECTIVE TUTORING

2ND EDITION

Ross B. MacDonald, Ph.D.

The Cambridge Stratford Study Skills Institute™

division of Cambridge Stratford, Ltd.

Williamsville, New York

TUTOR'S NAME _____

SUBJECT AREA _____

YEARS OF TUTORING
EXPERIENCE TO DATE _____

ABOUT THE AUTHOR

Dr. Ross B. MacDonald's expertise in tutoring and tutor training results from over ten years of research and experience. A nationally recognized authority, he speaks regularly at professional meetings. Over 400 tutoring professionals have learned from and appreciated his relaxed style and incisive analysis. The Master Tutor: A Guidebook for More Effective Tutoring is his latest effort. In the same incisive but relaxed style, he guides tutors through research-proven principles, strategies, and techniques of effective tutoring. He is currently developing evaluation instruments and procedures for tutor programs, including Tutor and Tutee Questionnaires. Supported by approximately $250,000 in grants, he has researched tutoring interaction and developed and tested training curriculum. In his most recent grant project, he directed the California Tutor Project, a consortium of 15 colleges. He holds BA and MA degrees in English and a Ph.D. in Instructional Communication. His research blends study in communication and teacher-student interaction. Dr. MacDonald is Director of the Science and Society Program at the University of California at Davis.

ABOUT THE PUBLISHER

The CAMBRIDGE STRATFORD STUDY SKILLS INSTITUTE is an international organization of learning skills and tutor training professionals dedicated to the pursuit of helping students of all ages to STUDY SMARTER, READ FASTER and SCORE HIGHER on TESTS, key ingredients for success in school as well as in life.

As a division of Cambridge Stratford, Ltd., the INSTITUTE provides inservice training and consulting to teaching staff plus formal instruction for students and tutors in the middle school through college levels using the internationally renowned editions of the Cambridge Stratford Study Skills Course (10 hour*, 20 hour, 30 hour; grades 6-13) and The Master Student: A Guidebook for More Effective Tutoring. (10 hour edition available in Spanish)

Library of Congress Number: 00-133398
ISBN: 0-935-637-27-3
2nd Printing © 2000
Printed in the USA

ACKNOWLEDGEMENTS

This book is dedicated to my wife, Patricia Harrison MacDonald.

I am also grateful to the many people who have helped me learn about tutoring. First mention in this regard belongs to the hundreds of tutors and tutees who let me observe and record their sessions. I have guaranteed them anonymity and so cannot name them. Second are the participants of the California Tutor Project: Daleen Chapman, Madison Cooper, Phyllis Cunningham, Anitra Dark, Dolores Dinneen, Bonnie Easley, Martin Jue, Evangeline Meneses, Maranda Montgomery, Felix Peréz, Debbie Rodriguez, Pat Tognozzi, Dorothy Williams, and John Wood.

I am also indebted to Dr. Ned Flanders and Dr. Susan Shimanoff for their insightful guidance and their high standards. Martha Maxwell encouraged me early and often. She finally said, "This book needs to be written and you need to do it." Finally, Peter Stevens believed in this book enough to publish and promote it.

To all of you who helped, thank you.

Approved for training and certification by The National Tutoring Association.

Graphic Artist Contribution: Ruth Santee, Tutor Training Coordinator
St. Mary's College of California
pp. 3, 79, 81, 87-88, and 108

PREFACE

Imagine two tutors reflecting on their first semester of tutoring. One tutor is frustrated, tired, and depressed. He spent hours during the term helping the same students with the same recurring problems. These students seem to rely continually on him. The other tutor was content, energetic, and pleased. She received several "thank you" cards, watched a number of her students improve their course performance, and saw significant changes in her students' attitudes towards school. Situations such as this occur frequently. How can it be that one tutor can be so up and the other so down?

Tutors, when well informed about tutoring more effectively, are consistently able to usefully apply strategies appropriate to each situation. Those who are well informed are energized by their tutees' improvement and satisfied with their tutoring. They know the most effective routes to helping tutees be able to succeed beyond tutoring. The Master Tutor: A Guidebook for More Effective Tutoring guides any tutor toward the immense satisfaction of helping others help themselves. The strategies and techniques are proven methods for master tutoring which produce more personal benefits with less stress.

If you are a tutor or a tutor trainer and you have many demands on your time, then this book is for you. It doesn't matter whether you are a "rookie" or a "grizzled veteran," this book will directly improve the quality of your tutoring and indirectly improve the quality of your school life. It doesn't matter whether you work in a tutoring center, an individual classroom, a peer advisement center, an after school program, or a summer workshop, this book will guide you to be better than you already are. It doesn't matter whether you help middle school students or graduate school students, The Master Tutor: A Guidebook For More Effective Tutoring is right on target.

ORIGIN OF THE MASTER TUTOR

Separating this book from any other on tutor training is its considerable research base that includes my experience as Director of The California Tutor Project, a 2 year pilot project composed of 15 colleges and hundreds of tutors and tutees. Therefore, this book is not based on somebody's educated guess about effective tutoring, nor is it based on what a committee decides should be taught. Instead, it is based on solid, systematic research conducted over several years. This book is derived from observations and analysis of hundreds of tutoring sessions and from analysis of the largest existing data base of tutor and tutee self-evaluations. An important result of the research is this Guidebook. The Master Tutor: A Guidebook for More Effective Tutoring contains a proven curriculum which encourages tutees' independent learning and work skills, and a corresponding reduction of their dependence on tutoring. Specifically, this research which includes The California Tutor Project has shown that:

(a) through a clearer understanding of their roles, rights and responsibilities, tutors and tutees felt more comfortable with their tutoring sessions;

(b) tutors felt more guided and informed about how to achieve the goals of tutoring;

(c) tutors learned more effective communication skills for relating productively and positively with their tutees;

(d) tutors learned to more skillfully blend listening, questioning, and explaining skills;

(e) tutors felt better able to relate well with students from many backgrounds and circumstances.

The Master Tutor builds on this research by providing a complete guide to achieving these outcomes. Because it is based on research, we know it works. Because it is based on years of experience training both tutors and tutor trainers, we believe you will find it accessible, to the point, and indispensable. We sincerely hope you too will find similar results. Awaiting you is the satisfaction of being able to more effectively help others, the pride of a job done to your highest standards, and the pleasure of knowing that your school and your community is better for you having been there.

The Master Tutor works because it leads to tutees who are better learners, not tutees who get more answers from their tutors. It works because tutors, already busy with courses, homework and family concerns, can learn the principles of the Guidebook in a relatively short time and apply them effectively in their tutoring. Overriding everything in this book is a focus on tutoring responsibly: helping students master learning processes necessary for succeeding in any subject. Ultimately, your role as a tutor is to make the best decisions you can about directing each individual session toward this goal. There is no single method for more effective tutoring. However, there is an essential body of information which, once mastered, will improve the quality of your decisions, and the quality of your relationships with tutees' learning experiences.

USE OF THE MASTER TUTOR

This Guidebook is designed to teach you the techniques that were observed to improve tutee's independent work skills. Its step-by-step cumulative format will be most beneficial in a formal training program. It can be reinforced by engaging peer tutors in discussion and role play exercises.A seminar format design of 10-14 hours is ideal for this training.

Whatever the format, The Master Tutor is designed to help you tutor more effectively by assessing and building on your strengths. Its strategies are not new nor are they simply ideas or preferences. Instead they come from proven research. To most of you who have tutored before and already found success, they will confirm what you're doing right and add further dimension to your purpose. This addition will empower you to help other tutors understand the value of these approaches. By contributing your peer support, both privately and in training sessions, you will fine-tune these skills and move them to higher levels of competence. You may even be called upon to help train new tutors.

Some tutors, satisfied with their tutoring practices, may question the rational for further approaches. Examine the book, consider the content, and think about your tutoring experiences. The goal of The Master Tutor is not to change attitudes but to encourage an adjustment in practices. These adjustments will help you observe your tutee develop from hesitating at first, groping for information second, and taking charge third. Once you observe this result, you may discover the need to review some of the concepts covered to see what else could cause further and, even more beneficial, changes. With this possibility in mind, I ask you to be open-minded in approaching this Guidebook. In the note column added to the side of each page, be prepared with pen or marker to write thoughts and reactions next to provocative passages or exercises you read. These may prove important later on.

Regardless of your experience in tutoring, The Master Tutor will help you see how managing yourself in tutoring is the key to managing your tutee's problems. The plans, strategies, and techniques suggested will increase your effectiveness in helping tutees. These strategies are designed to encourage proven learning behavior, behavior that will get tutees to do more of their own work. Behavior that you'll recognize as similar to that used by all the good teachers who helped you get this far in your life.

TUTOR TRAINER'S NOTE

Tutor Trainers and coordinators will find The Master Tutor to sum up many of the bits and pieces you've learned over the years, and to encase them in a concise, streamlined and well-structured approach. Used independently by tutors, it can be read over the weekend and can serve as a discussion topic for your first orientation meeting. Used as a curriculum for more indepth training, it can help create a stimulating classroom seminar complete with role play exercises, observations and video critiques. The numerous exercises, self assessments and practice examples provided in the Guidebook help tutors to use the techniques in tutoring sessions as early as tomorrow. As such, The Master Tutor can be of great value to both newly recruited tutors who need an orientation to their role, and to seasoned tutors, even those often called upon to handle the more difficult tutoring situations.

Additionally, The Master Tutor is a time saver for you as well. Just as my earlier example of the different approaches of the two tutors in paragraph 1, you've probably tried a mixture of homespun and commercial approaches with mixed reactions. Sometimes, this resulted in having a lot of tutors coming back to you with similar problems time and time again. Building The Master Tutor into your curriculum can help streamline your training and make it easier and more effective for years to come. By using these techniques, seasoned tutors can begin to help new tutors understand the complexity of their tasks, and give them a clearer and more directed approach to those tasks. In a sense, The Master Tutor's benefits go far beyond your first training program. It establishes a self-supporting and self-perpetuating framework for training tutors. Some seasoned tutors may be able to become para-professional Tutor Trainers and augment your efforts.

Further help is available or being planned. A Tutor Trainer's Manual and Transparency Set have been published in a format designed for 10-14 hours of supplemental training. Other enhancements being planned include role playing video tapes, auditory cassettes and other supplements that further expand The Master Tutor into subject area tutoring. As you can understand, my intent goes beyond this Guidebook. It's a strong commitment to insuring the advancement of a discipline that, heretofore, has remained an invaluable, yet overlooked, component of our educational support system.

EVALUATION AND ASSESSMENT

Some tutors will have a penchant for monitoring their success with The Master Tutor's strategies. A pre/post assessment, entitled the TESAT (Tutor Evaluation and Self-Assessment Tool), has been published as a supplement to this guidbook. It provides two compilations over two time intervals of self-assessed scores by tutors based on their use of the strategies of The 12 Step Tutor Cycle (Chapter 2), namely before reading and/or training and after reading and/or training with The Mastor Tutor. Other evaluation is a built-in part of this guidebook. For example, you can ask tutees to rate the percentage of time they talked compared to you (i.e. balanced time). You can learn these techniques with the help of another tutor and rate your performance on completing each of the steps, use of options, patterns for talk or statements with biased implications. The fact is these strategies are easily observed and measured.

This has further implications for tutor trainers as well. Evaluation is a direct product of adopting the strategies of The Master Tutor. From simple role play observations to TUTOR/TUTEE QUESTIONAIRES, to comparing the results of student outcomes, The Master Tutor curriculum encourages evaluation before, during and after training commences. If your institution plans to explore these options, please let me know. I would like to help.

FINAL NOTE: A TUTOR'S PERSPECTIVE

I've written The Master Tutor to synthesize many difficult concepts into useful and understandable language. I've also written it with the perspective that empathizes with the frustrated tutor from the example in paragraph 1, the depressed one. Thus, I've tried to write in a style that talks to the mindset of the tutor. I believe this makes the experiences and exercises presented more interesting, evocative and thought provoking. My goal is to inspire you to a new way of thinking, performing and acting. My experience with training tutors has shaped my insights on how far we can go in making the tutor/tutee interaction more effective and efficient. A 5% change in you can often cause a 50% change in the student you tutor. When you realize this, you will want to explore further ways to effect even more change among the students you tutor. These strategies are currently available. They are only limited by our decisions to use them. I hope The Master Tutor helps you try.

A 5% change in you can often cause a 50% change in the student you tutor. When you realize this, you will want to explore further ways to effect even more change among the students you tutor.

THE MASTER TUTOR: A GUIDEBOOK FOR MORE EFFECTIVE TUTORING

TABLE OF CONTENTS

INTRODUCTION

WELCOME!

You either are a tutor or thinking of becoming one. Being a tutor is likely to both challenge you and reward you in profound ways. No doubt you'll have students you'll find easy to tutor, but you'll also have students who will test all of your skills. Clearly the fact that you have been recruited as a tutor indicates that professionals at your school believe that you are up to this challenge. Although you likely have some concerns about your potential as a tutor, you probably feel that you can handle it. Good! This Guidebook helps you meet the challenge.

Your Tutoring Is Important

As a tutor, you are an important part of an extraordinary development in education. Tutoring has been shown to be an effective intervention for students who are at risk of failing or performing poorly in school. In over 70% of our nation's colleges and in a good portion of our high schools, tutoring services are available to students, often at no charge. Tutoring is of particular significance because in the last 25 years, more students from diverse backgrounds are seeking social, economic, and personal attainment through educational achievement. Many of these students need help knowing how to succeed. Knowing less about how the school "game" is played and having fewer resources in their lives, they are at greater risk of dropping out or not achieving up to their abilities. It is primarily for these students that tutoring has been developed.

I intend to guide you toward tutoring excellence and to thus enhance your feelings of competence and confidence. This Guidebook provides you with state of the art knowledge about tutoring developed from years of intensive research and many experiences training thousands of tutors and hundreds of tutor trainers from schools all over North America. I have seen profound evidence of the benefits of tutoring many, many times. I still am thrilled when the light bulb goes on and people's eyes light up. By writing this book and sharing what I've learned with you, I hope to contribute to and share in your successes in tutoring.

A Guidebook

This is a Guidebook, not a "how to" book. A "how to" book suggests some foolproof method of doing something. Let's think about that for a minute. FOOLPROOF. This suggests arrogance and condescension at the same time. It seems arrogant to state that there's one right way to raise your kids, attract a mate, lose weight, get in shape, win friends and influence people, or tutor another human being. Foolproof seems condescending because of the name. The word foolproof says that even if you're a fool, you can't mess *this* up. You're not a fool, however, and neither are your potential tutees. You are needed for your sensitivity and your abilities. A book such as this can guide you to applying your sensitivity and your abilities to tutoring effectively, but it can't give you a complete script for tutoring. Effective tutoring results from informed and sensitive decisions, decisions which have to be made quickly and smoothly. Tutors or program developers looking for a foolproof, single approach to all tutoring situations are ignoring the richly diverse array of human experience and the resulting complex character of human interaction.

Each tutoring session is its own entity. It has its own characteristics, its own flavor, its own life. While there are certain components to effective tutoring encounters, there is an infinite variety in the complexion and interweaving of these components. As you and the tutee create a tutoring encounter, you will be making countless moment-to-moment decisions affecting the direction of the tutoring and the quality of the tutoring relationship. Training is therefore critically important to helping you make good decisions and being an effective tutor.

MAKING GOOD DECISIONS

Your effectiveness as a decision maker will result from a synthesis of four factors: (1) your *commitment* to becoming a MASTER TUTOR, (2) your *knowledge about tutoring*; (3) your *knowledge of the subjects* you tutor; and (4) your *interpersonal skills*. Your successful synthesis of these four factors enables you to make good decisions when you tutor. Please don't take this commitment lightly. There is a body of information for you to know. More importantly, learning to be a MASTER TUTOR will require that you change some of the ways you might normally communicate or think about others. Making changes in your behavior and in your thinking is not easy. It can be unsettling, but it can be done. Many before you have done it.

In turn, I am committed to giving you the information you need to be a MASTER TUTOR. This Guidebook is based on research — proven knowledge — not speculation. This Guidebook is practical, not abstract. This Guidebook contains only essential information, not everything anybody can think of about tutoring. Further, this information is useful for whatever subjects you tutor.

If you and I are successful, then you will be a MASTER TUTOR, you will have the time you need to do your own school work, and you will be your own best evaluator of your effectiveness as a tutor.

INTRODUCTION ▮▮▮▮▮▮

ORIENTATION TO THE BOOK

HOW THIS BOOK IS ORGANIZED

Notes: ♕

Probably the first thing you have already noticed is that this book is written in a casual tone. The book doesn't read like the usual textbook. A textbook intends to organize and present knowledge: factually, objectively, and academically. Few textbook authors intend to guide their readers on a personal journey. This is a different kind of a book with a different purpose. I have imagined that I am talking with you. I am trying to guide you to mastery of tutoring and intend to develop a relationship with you.

Five chapters. The book is divided into five chapters: the tutoring role, the tutoring cycle, tutoring options, tutoring patterns, and tutoring inter-culturally. The first chapter defines the mission and basic goals of tutoring and helps you learn how to stay within them. The second chapter presents a series of steps which make up tutoring. Of particular importance are steps promoting students' understanding about how to learn that which is giving them trouble. If they understand how to learn, then they become more able and more independent. In the third chapter, you will learn about the six options available to you as a tutor. These options help you make decisions about how to communicate with tutees.

The fourth chapter is the shortest. You'll need a short chapter after the third! It explains the two basic communication patterns found in tutoring and discusses the advantages and disadvantages of each. The final chapter intends to help you develop a broader framework for working with people from all backgrounds. We are all in some ways different from each other: the greater the difference between two people, the greater the likelihood of misunderstanding. This chapter intends to reduce misunderstanding by showing the role of culture in communication processes and helping you be able to see outside of the framework of your culture.

Notes: ✍

FEATURES OF THE GUIDEBOOK

<u>Organizing logos.</u> Each chapter has a simple logo representing it in one of five boxes. They are on the next page.

There is a logo for each chapter. The first chapter concerns goals. The star is intended to suggest these goals. The cyclical nature of the second graphic represents the tutoring cycle. The question mark in the third box represents the options for tutor talk. The two arrows in the fourth box suggest the two patterns of tutoring interaction. The oval in the box surrounded by diagonal lines suggests a person's head and the cultural framework from which we perceive and communicate.

As you begin a chapter, you will see a graphic in the box for that chapter in the upper corner. As you move through the text, each chapter's graphic will appear in the appropriate box. Thus, in the first chapter only the first graphic shows in its box. In the second chapter, the second graphic will be highlighted. At the beginning of each chapter, all the boxes will be displayed and will begin to form a sequence depicting the connection of the five parts of <u>The Master Tutor</u>.

The graphics serve three purposes. First, each graphic suggests the central idea of that chapter. By seeing the graphic regularly, I hope to help you internalize the central concept. Second, because they appear in the upper corner of every page, the graphics help you easily locate sections of the book for study or further review. Third, adding graphics as you move through the chapters signals your progress through the book.

<u>Exercises and situations.</u> In each chapter you will find exercises for you to complete. Signaled by a shaded box, they extend or reinforce concepts and give you practice in applying what you learn. The self-assessments at the end of this chapter are examples of exercises.

Other shaded boxes are used to highlight sample situations not calling for a written response but requiring your careful thought. These situations provide practical dramatizations of significant issues in tutoring. All situations are based on real incidents unless indicated otherwise. Names have been changed.

<u>Notes in the margin.</u> Down the outside margin of each page is a blank space. This gives you a place to write notes, questions, comments, pictures, and so forth. I encourage you to take advantage of this space. Relevant writing, drawing, even some doodling helps you understand and retain information.

<u>Other features of the text.</u> You will also note that I sometimes use bold or *italic print*. Bold print signals new concepts and their definitions. *Italic print* is for emphasis.

Headings help you see the hierarchical organization of the material.

Organizing Features of The Master Tutor:

A Guidebook for More Effective Tutoring

Notes: ✍

Centered headings signal the largest division. What you are reading now comes under the main heading, "Orientation to the Book." Secondary headings at the left margin which stand alone represent subcategories of the centered headings (see for example the heading for this section, Features of the Guidebook). Underlined text at the beginning of a paragraph are the smallest divisions (see for example <u>Other features of the text</u> at the beginning of the previous paragraph).

Before we proceed with the rest of the book, please complete the two assessment questionnaires which follow. The first questionnaire assesses your knowledge about tutoring. The second asks you to assess your interpersonal skills.

These assessments will be repeated at the end of your training to help you evaluate your understanding of the central themes of The Master Tutor curriculum for helping you become a more effective tutor.

EXERCISE: ASSESS YOUR KNOWLEDGE

Notes: ✍

The following questionnaire tests your understanding of tutoring. Indicate whether each statement is true or false by placing a "T" or an "F" on the line.

_____ 1. It's my role to help my students with whatever they need help with. (Ch. 1)

_____ 2. If a tutee I work with doesn't get the information, then I am responsible. (Ch. 1)

_____ 3. I know that I will encounter some students who have no motivation. (Ch. 1)

_____ 4. If I feel that I have been assigned to work with a student whose needs are beyond my ability to help, then I should tell my supervisor right away. (Ch. 1)

_____ 5. At the beginning of every tutoring session, the tutor and I should plan the session and set an agenda for it, even if it takes two or three minutes. (Ch. 2)

_____ 6. I would expect that in tutoring sessions, tutees should do more explaining than their tutors. (Ch. 3)

_____ 7. It's critically important that I praise my tutees liberally. (Ch. 3)

_____ 8. Providing clear and accurate explanations to the tutee is at the heart of my best tutoring. (Ch. 3 and 4)

_____ 9. Asking good questions is at the heart of my best tutoring. (Ch. 3 and 4)

_____ 10. Compared to me, at least some of the students I work with are likely to have very different attitudes toward school and the subjects I tutor. (Ch. 5)

_____ 11. It's important for me to trust my perceptions. (Ch. 5)

_____ 12. My students must learn standard English and I should teach them. (Ch. 5)

_____ TOTAL CORRECT   *Answers on following page*

EXERCISE: ASSESS YOUR KNOWLEDGE   Answers

1. False 2. False 3. False 4. True 5. True 6. True 7. False 8. False 9. False 10. True 11. False 12. False

So how did you do? In this next exercise, you will assess your skills. In this exercise there are no right answers, just your own self-evaluation. Both the skill assessment and the knowledge assessment reoccur in the conclusion, providing you the opportunity to gauge for yourself some of the effects of the training you will receive.

EXERCISE: ASSESS YOUR SKILLS

Rate yourself on each statement. Place the appropriate number on the line at the front of the statement.

1: strongly agree 2: agree 3: neither agree nor disagree
4: disagree 5: strongly disagree

____ 1. I am committed to being a good tutor.
____ 2. I am able to objectively evaluate myself.
____ 3. People would generally say I am a good listener.
____ 4. I can explain to others how to learn the subjects I tutor.
____ 5. I am able to explain the same idea in several different ways.
____ 6. I have a repertoire of skills for communicating effectively with others.
____ 7. I am open to new ideas and new perspectives.
____ 8. I have the sensitivity and self-awareness to understand how I am different from each of my tutees.
____ 9. I am able to adjust my tutoring according to the individual characteristics of my tutees.
____ 10. At this point I understand how to tutor successfully.

I wish you enjoyable, productive tutoring experiences. I welcome your comments and suggestions. I am also very interested in your interesting, puzzling, or unusual tutoring experiences. Please send them to me care of the publisher whose address is listed on a printed "Dear Dr. MacDonald" form at the end of this guidebook. I promise to write back to you promptly.

INTRODUCTION

CHAPTER 1:
TUTOR ROLE

 TUTORING ROLE

 TUTORING CYCLE

 TUTORING OPTIONS

 TUTORING PATTERNS

 TUTORING INTER- CULTURALLY

CHAPTER 1: TUTOR ROLE

INTRODUCTION

Congratulations! If you are reading this book, it's likely that you are a tutor or about to become one. But wait a minute! What is a tutor? Thinking about this important question will enrich your experiences and help you avoid some common pitfalls. As you think about what a tutor is, incorporate information from at least these three sources: this Guidebook, your tutor training class, and your own learning experiences. Although your sense of your role as a tutor will continue to evolve, for now, keep in mind that a tutor fills a very specific role within a school and that staying within that role gives you and the students you assist the best chance for satisfaction and success in tutoring. Discussion of the tutoring role is intended to help you understand what is appropriate for tutoring, help you recognize situations which can lead you out of the appropriate role, and help you react effectively to inappropriate requests.

REALITY CHECK

Does talking about your role seem like an abstract exercise not related to the day-to-day realities of tutoring? If so, consider these situations which real tutors like yourselves have grappled with. Except for the fact that names have been changed, these situations are true.

The situations are designed to stimulate thought and discussion. Each of you will see these differences in a slightly different light. We all flesh out the situations according to our individual experiences and expectations. This is particularly important when we imagine tutors and tutees to be of different backgrounds. Differences in age, ethnicity, social standing, educational attainments, and so forth can profoundly influence how we interpret and understand individual situations. Chapter 5 is specifically addressed to what is arguably the most important component of this training guidebook: tutoring inter-culturally. For now, please focus on what you can learn from your peers' interpretations as well as on your own.

After each situation, write your reaction of what you would say if you were the tutor faced with the problem described. Specifically, what do you think?: a) What is the problem? and b) What should the tutor do about it?

Situation 1: "Helpful." Lisa, a sociology tutor at a medium sized college, meets with one of the students from the class, Paul, to discuss his progress on an important writing assignment for the introductory course. Lisa begins to discuss the essay with Paul. She believes some parts are quite well written and others are rather poorly done. Paul explains that he has been working with Angela, a cheery and helpful tutor for the same class. He has been very pleased with Angela, as she has "really helped him write several passages." Lisa slowly learns that the strong passages are really mostly written by a too-helpful Angela. Lisa attempts to draw Paul into writing and revising his own paper, but he wants her to suggest language. Pen poised, he says, somewhat accusingly, "Why don't you help me like Angela does?"

How would you react to Paul? (Write your reaction below)

1. What is the problem? _____

2. What should the tutor do about it? _____

_____

_____

"Why don't you help me like Angela does?"

Notes:

Situation 2: "Nervous." Francisco has been tutoring Maria for one hour in each of the last five weeks at a community college in California. They have developed a strong rapport and are productively engaged in helping Maria with her Introduction to Psychology class. At the beginning of their meeting on this, the sixth week of their tutoring, Maria arrives late and looks very shaken. Her eyes dart about nervously, her body is constantly in motion, she's even wringing her hands. Francisco has known that Maria is a little nervous, but this is definitely much more than that. Francisco expresses concern. Maria blurts, "My shrink changed my medication and I didn't like it so I stopped taking it. I am really having trouble feeling OK right now." It dawns on Francisco that Maria may be talking about medication related to psychological treatment. Maria begins to describe the situation in more depth but her narrative is very disjointed and the more she talks the more she becomes agitated. Francisco knows their tutoring time is ticking away.

How would you react to Maria? (Write your reaction below)

1. What is the problem? _____

2. What should the tutor do about it? _____

_____

_____

_____

_____

_____

TUTOR ROLE

Notes:

Situation 3: "Great Expectations." Kevin greatly admires his economics teacher, Mr. Hoover. He is dynamic, forceful, funny (in a sarcastic way), inspirational, and very confident of his knowledge. When Mr. Hoover recruited Kevin to be a tutor he was thrilled initially and enthusiastically joined the school's tutoring program. However, early in his first semester of tutoring, Mr. Hoover meets with Kevin. Mr. Hoover explains that he doesn't waste time on struggling students and he doesn't want Kevin to either. He says, "Look, the kids who aren't getting A's and B's aren't going anywhere anyway. I just focus on the good students and I want you to do the same. And as long as you won't be wasting your time on those students, you can correct tests for me and we'll let the tutoring center pay for it. We just won't tell the center we're doing this." Mr. Hoover then goes on to describe how much fun he has sarcastically putting down struggling students. He seems to want Kevin to laugh as well.

How would you react to Mr. Hoover? (Write your reaction below)

1. What is the problem? _____

2. What should the tutor do about it? _____

_____

_____

_____

_____

_____

_____

In each case, what you thought was the problem and what the tutor should do about it probably derived from what your instincts and experience told you. Now consider the information presented in this next section and reflect on these situations afterward.

WHAT IS A TUTOR?

A tutor is a person who, in a structured and supervised educational context, enters into a peer teaching and learning relationship with one or more others. Let's take a brief look at the important components of this definition. **Structured and supervised educational context** means that tutoring occurs as part of some program which is a designated educational service. In other words, your tutoring is sanctioned by the school as is your school bookstore, athletic teams, math classes, and cafeteria. For each of these programs, including tutoring, your school takes responsibility for such things as time and place of operation, supervision and support of personnel, and coordination with other school activities. **Peer** means that you are at approximately the same grade level in school as the students you tutor.

A **teaching and learning relationship** means that you and your tutees develop ways of communicating and ways of being together which fit the purpose of teaching and learning. Thus, a tutoring relationship can be distinguished from a close friend relationship, a worker/supervisor relationship, a doctor/patient relationship, and so forth. So in the definition above, we're using the term teaching in the broadest sense. **Teaching** is any act which facilitates or provides a structure for another's learning. **Learning** is defined as acquiring knowledge. While you are the one primarily teaching, you will be learning a great deal. Similarly, while the tutee is primarily learning, he/she will be teaching you a great deal. As you will see in the tutoring goals section later in this chapter, **tutoring is a specialized kind of instruction significantly different than traditional teaching.** We'll use the term **tutee** to designate the students whom you tutor.

ANALYSIS OF SITUATIONS

In Situation #1: "Helpful," Paul has learned that tutors do some of the students' work and is getting upset that Lisa is operating under a different assumption. Lisa is torn between wanting to be helpful, not wanting to do the students' work, and wondering about the tutoring Paul received from Angela. Lisa is right to not do Paul's work.

TUTOR ROLE

Similarly, in Situation #2: "Nervous," Maria needs help coping with her agitation and anxiety, but Francisco is not a therapist and so cannot responsibly help Maria with her personal relationships. Theirs is a tutoring relationship, not a client/therapist one.

Situation #3: "Great Expectations," illustrates another and even more complicated entangling of relationships. Kevin is being asked to be a tutor, but also to focus exclusively on the more successful students. Worse, he is being implicitly asked to join his teacher in making fun of less successful students. Complicating matters further, what's at stake for both Kevin and Mr. Hoover is a mentor/mentee relationship. If Kevin participates in making fun of students, he maintains his place as a "special student." He also corrupts the tutoring relationship. On the other hand, if Kevin resists the pull to ridicule students, he may lose his relationship with Mr. Hoover. Adding even another dimension of complication, Kevin's role as employee of the tutoring center requires him to receive pay for tutoring time only. To do otherwise is to violate the employer/employee relationship. Kevin is in a bad spot because roles are in conflict.

These situations and others like them occur frequently in tutoring. Analyzing them is useful for two reasons. First, these situations alert you to what could happen at some time in your tutoring experience. Second, they provide a useful, practical focus for thinking about your role as a tutor, especially its limits. If Kevin, Francisco, and Lisa fulfill the expectations placed on them, they will go beyond the role of a tutor. You can see the problems which will likely result. Kevin will be taking money from the tutoring program under false circumstances, making ridiculing remarks, and not helping a set of students; Francisco will be counseling a distraught Maria; and Lisa will be doing Paul's work.

Situations such as these threaten to take you out of your role as a tutor.

DIFFERENCES BETWEEN TEACHING AND TUTORING

As discussed earlier in this chapter, in the broad sense what tutors do and what teachers do is teach. However, tutoring is a specialized kind of teaching. Further, many of the advantages of tutoring derive from the differences between the tutor role and the teacher role. Tutors are different from teachers in at least the following areas: training, job responsibilities, term of employment, compensation, status, and relationship to school.

Notes:

Notes:

Teachers have at least a bachelor's degree. Most college teachers possess a master's or doctorate, giving them in-depth knowledge in the field in which they teach. Tutors are usually still in school. Teachers are paid full time salaries and are employed for a career.

Teachers are responsible for all business related to instructing assigned groups of students: curriculum development, instructional plans, homework and test preparation and correction, recordkeeping, and so forth. Compared to teachers, your role as a tutor is narrower, your responsibilities fewer, your pay lower, and your status different! What you do is important, it's just not the same as what a teacher does. Your job is thankfully less complex. Your role is best defined by understanding what your goals are.

SIX GOALS OF TUTORING

Goals are general statements of desired long range outcomes. The goals of tutoring indicate what tutors *do*. If you stay focused on these goals of tutoring, then you will be within your role as a tutor. The six goals are to:

1. promote independence in learning;
2. personalize instruction;
3. facilitate tutee insights into learning and learning processes;
4. provide a student perspective on learning and school success;
5. respect individual differences; and
6. follow a job description.

The following discussion briefly elaborates on each of these goals.

PROMOTE INDEPENDENT LEARNING

The first goal is to act in ways which promote and respect students' independence. Students want to be able to do things on their own and it's your job to help make that happen. Students seek tutoring because they feel they need additional help with a given course. *In turn, a tutor helps students in ways that make students better able to help themselves and in ways that reduce their need for continual help.* When tutees feel that they themselves have the ability to gain knowledge, they are empowered. The resulting feelings of confidence and self-reliance, coupled with an increase in knowing how to learn, enables tutees to successfully tackle new learning tasks. They come to believe that the power to succeed is within them. Thus, there is a basic irony in tutoring: **you are working to create your own obsolescence**. You help tutees in ways which reduce their need for your future help. Let me provide you with an example from my own experience.

Pottery example. I once enrolled in a pottery class at the local adult night school. Using rotating pottery wheels, our task was to slowly "pull a pot" from a carefully arranged lump of wet clay plopped in the exact middle of the wheel. The skill of pottery making is in pulling a pot which is graceful, tall, and thin-walled. Any mistake and another stubby ashtray is made. I made a lot of ashtrays until one day I began to "pull" a pot. The "force" was with me. A firm but stable pressure between my thumbs on the inside and my fingers on the outside was yielding clay walls which were symmetrical. A pot was happening! The teacher noted my success and stood right behind me.

TUTOR ROLE

Suddenly her hands were on mine and she increasingly exerted pressure on the clay, slowly but steadily taking over the process. Her words of encouragement were gutted by her actions. Her statements, "There, uh huh, it's coming, nice shape," were more a commentary on the result she was engineering than on anything I was doing. I felt cheated. I knew *she* could make a pot. She'd demonstrated her easy competence many times. This time, *I* had been making one. "Had been" because I removed my hands from the wheel, keenly aware of the difference between her pottery skills and mine. She finished and congratulated *me*! "There! Look at your pot!" "Not mine," I muttered and walked away.

The teacher attained her desired result. A good pot was crafted. However, her instructional process (putting her hands on my pot) made me feel less able. What had started out as my work was mine no longer. In addition, I was even more aware of the difference between her level of competency and mine. **She inadvertently trained dependence and discouragement, rather than independence and empowerment.**

Provide opportunity. Your goal as a tutor is to provide students the opportunity to do their work. The focus is on how to do it more than on getting it done. So, can you get the tutee to stand at the chalkboard writing things down? For math tutoring, ensure that the student holds the pencil and tries to solve the equation. In English composition, allow the student to write corrections on his essay. **Providing opportunity** is a dominant theme in this text and, for the most effective tutors, is a dominant theme in their tutoring.

PERSONALIZE INSTRUCTION

Personalizing instruction refers to a tutor's unique position to structure a learning encounter to a particular individual. Compared to teacher-led classrooms with thirty or more students, tutors work one-on-one or one-on-small group, can pace activities to suit the tutees, can utilize examples particularly relevant or drawn from the experiences of the individuals being tutored, can more easily elicit and attend closely to tutees' ideas, and can more closely follow and anticipate student progress. Personalizing instruction in these ways greatly increases the likelihood that students will learn the material.

We know that as people connect what they're learning to what they already know, they learn more readily and retain what they learn for a longer period of time. Tutors are in a wonderful position to help students relate learning to personal experiences and thus learn more and retain it longer.

Learning strategies. Further, tutors have an opportunity to closely monitor students' learning and can thus help improve and reinforce those learning strategies which are most productive. The term **learning strategy** denotes a plan of action for accomplishing a specific learning goal. Amazingly, although helping students with learning strategies is an essential function of tutoring, it is usually overlooked. *Helping students improve their learning strategies is the most direct route to promoting independence and empowerment.* The importance of learning strategies and how to tutor them is covered in more depth in Chapter 2: The Tutoring Cycle, especially in the discussions of Steps #4 and #8. For now, if you focus your tutoring on the tutee's learning strategies, then you become a facilitator, one who *aids* another's efforts; you are not an explainer, one who *tells* another; nor are you a surrogate, one who *does* for another.

FACILITATE TUTEE INSIGHTS

It is not *your* discovery of answers which is the goal of tutoring. Your goal is to work with students in such a way that *they* discover answers. When you accomplish this goal, you are facilitating. **To facilitate is to provide opportunities and support to others so they can do good things**. Facilitators establish an environment for others to do good work by removing potential obstacles and offering additional resources and tools to assist the work. The process of making it easier for students to do their own work can therefore be distinguished from the process of doing students' work for them.   It's true that in the short term, doing the student's work is efficient because you can do it faster than the tutee; moreover, you can certainly do it faster yourself than you can help the tutee learn how to do it. In the long term, however, doing the student's work is very inefficient. The student will continue to need your help with all related work. While facilitating the student's learning takes more of your time and skill in the short term, it will be more efficient in the long run. The student will gain the ability and necessary self-confidence to learn independently of you.

When James, a Chem 1A student, says, "I don't know how to diagram this chemical compound," you will likely to be tempted to say, "Here, let me show you." While well-intentioned, this approach, whether in Chem 1A or in pottery class, does not facilitate the student's learning. Instead, it

Notes:

substitutes your learning for his as you do his work for him. And if you do his work for him, what will happen the next time he encounters a similar task? Right. He'll come to you first.

<u>How to facilitate</u>. To *facilitate* you might say to the Chem 1A student, "Well, how would you start?" This keeps the power to do the work in James' hands and will help you discover what obstacles are in his way. When you say, "Here let me show you," you are doing the student's work. When you say, "Well, how would you start?" you are facilitating. James can take the lead in explaining how to diagram the chemical compound. Remember that it is James' learning which is the focus in this tutoring situation, not yours. Further, when you ask James about how he will proceed, you reinforce the importance of his learning strategies. Thus, not only are you helping James take the lead in his tutoring with you, but you are helping him develop learning strategies and giving him guided practice in using them.

PROVIDE A STUDENT PERSPECTIVE

You as a tutor have a kind of credibility and rapport with a student that is much more difficult for a teacher to attain. Your rapport derives from the fact that, like your tutees, you are a student. From the tutees' perspective, this makes you one of us (students) not one of them (teachers or professors). You have to buy books, scramble for classes you need, park in distant or muddy parking lots or travel circuitous public transit routes, pay tuition and fees, wait in lines for services, and suffer all the other minor indignities of being a student. Further, from the tutee's perspective, your talk and appearance identify you as a student.

Your credibility derives from the fact that you are a successful student. You must be successful given that you are a tutor and that you got through Higgenbottom's Chemistry 1A class with a good grade. Based on recent personal experience, therefore, you have insight about how to be a successful student in the class for which your tutees need help. From the tutee's perspective, in other words, you are one of them and you have valuable inside knowledge about getting through a troublesome class.

RESPECT INDIVIDUAL DIFFERENCES

Notes:

You are likely to be working with students whose backgrounds are in some ways different from yours. Some tutees will be quite different. You have valuable insights to give and a valuable service to provide. It is important to understand that your approach to school and learning, the kinds of experiences you have had with people in school, the degree of support you receive directly and implicitly from your family and community, your financial circumstances, and so forth <u>are not all the same</u> as that of the students you work with. In addition, it is essential for you to remember that people who are different than you are not in some way flawed or inferior.

In this text an entire chapter is devoted to this subject: Tutoring Interculturally. *You can refer to the chapter on inter-cultural tutoring at any time in your training.* For now, we'll focus on your responsibilities and the limits of your responsibilities.

Maintaining respect for students may be most difficult when your tutoring with someone is not going well. In such a case, tutors sometimes say things like, "he's unmotivated," or "she just doesn't care," or "he's just not getting it." The focus of these statements is the student, some one else. We all tend to do this to save our self-images. Not being able to do something well is threatening to our self-image. When you are confronted with a student who seems to not be doing well, *you may find it easier to focus on what the student is not doing than to focus on what your tutoring is not doing.* Further, what we recognize in others and how we tutor them is sometimes based on a set of false assumptions about what a good student looks like, acts like, talks like, and so forth.

<u>The issue of motivation</u>. Sometimes when a student does not seem to be progressing well, a tutor will complain that the student is "unmotivated." Let's think about this for a minute. Let's examine the claim that a student is unmotivated.

The first feature of an unmotivated allegation is the assumption that motivation is a fixed character trait. That like eye color, motivation doesn't change. A second assumption is that motivation is a yes or no trait: you either have it or you don't. A third assumption is that the tutor can somehow accurately assess motivation. Each assumption is false. For example, a person who is truly unmotivated would never get out of bed, much less go to school or seek out a tutor

Motivation results from internalized feelings of success at meaningful tasks. The more success, the higher the motivation. The more one internalizes the belief of success, the more one will feel it. The result is that a person is more likely to take on similar tasks and to have confidence about chances for success. It is this set of feelings which defines motivation. Assessment of motivation is therefore a complex psychological process. It's likely none of us is sufficiently trained and experienced to make that assessment.

<u>Your responsibility.</u> Your job is to approach each tutoring session with your best efforts. If things aren't going well, ask yourself why and avoid the temptation to immediately blame the student. It could be that once you understand and respect the differences between you and the student, you will be much more successful. You are responsible for giving each session your best effort. Part of doing this is to structure the tutoring so that the student does have success at a task: real success at a meaningful task.

When things don't go well, the system can help you. There are people at your school who can be resources for you. Your tutor trainer and your supervisor are at the top of the list of resources. Discuss the situation with them. You can also seek advice from a trusted teacher. Find ways to change your approach so that the student can experience success.

<u>Limits of your responsibility</u>. However, you are not ultimately responsible for whether that student succeeds. That is the student's responsibility. Focus on doing your job well and you will avoid issues of blame. Blame is a *symptom* of an unsatisfactory situation.

Finally, make sure you aren't being asked to do the impossible. Unfortunately the system sometimes works in ways which present tutors with dilemmas such as this. You should not try to solve these dilemmas by continuing to tutor. No tutor, for example, can responsibly bridge the gap between a student who reads at the fourth grade level and the requirements of a college literature class. You may be asked to tutor a student because nobody else knew what to do with that student. The teacher didn't know, the counselor didn't know, so they send the student to a tutor — maybe to you. This is a disservice to you and the student. If something such as this should happen to you, consult your tutor supervisor or your trainer immediately. Someone may respond by telling you to "just do the best you can." Be firm. Explain that the gap is just too large for you to bridge.

FOLLOW YOUR JOB DESCRIPTION

As an employee of your school, you are bound by a job description and school policy. While there are differences among schools as to the function of a tutor, most responsible, well-organized tutoring programs define the tutoring job as helping students individually or in small groups. Tutors are paid or receive credit for tutoring and for any record-keeping directly related

TUTOR ROLE

to the job. If you have no written job description, meet with your supervisor to review carefully what is expected of you.

 Notes:

LIMITS OF THE TUTOR'S ROLE

As was illustrated in the three situations earlier in this chapter, many tutors feel an obligation to help tutees or instructors with issues outside the scope of the classes for which the tutees sought tutoring. Like the rest of the world, students have trouble with family relations, unexpected medical problems, emotional traumas, financial resources, and so forth. Although not very likely, it's still possible that you as a tutor will hear of a problem as profound as date rape, unexpected death in the immediate family, impending bankruptcies, sexual harassment by school personnel or students, or racially motivated personal attacks. More likely, you may hear of problems as mundane as lost or stolen textbooks, expensive parking tickets, difficult course registration processes, or inconsiderate roommates. Most tutors never encounter the dramatic problems, but a few will. On the other hand, many tutors encounter the more mundane problems. In either case, it's important to be prepared. The best preparation is to know what your role is — to be very sure of what is expected of you.

CLEARLY OUT OF BOUNDS

In the abstract, most tutors can easily see that personal problems, while significant and important, are outside the range of the tutor role — and out of the range of a tutor's expertise. But when one of these abstract problems unexpectedly has an immediate focus on Maria's face, a tutee you have come to know and regard over several weeks of tutoring, then it is often more difficult to remain within the scope of your tutoring role. This dilemma was illustrated in Situations #1 and #2 earlier in the chapter. Consider a fourth situation, only now you are the tutor.

Situation #4: "It Hits Home." Your tutee, Matthew, whom you have tutored once a week for the past five weeks, arrives looking agitated and upset. You express concern. He tells you he is "very hurt and angry" because his parents have cut off all support for his college. The reason: last weekend he told his parents that he is gay and they have responded by cutting off all support. You didn't know he was gay either. According to Matthew, they feel that "school has made me this way." He says to you, "You've always been really understanding and helpful with my school work. What should I do?"

Notes:

How would you react to Matthew? (Write your reaction below)

1. What is the problem? _____

2. What should the tutor do about it? _____

_____

_____

Dr. Kronick, DDS. What do you say to Matthew? Before you answer, consider this analogy. Imagine Dr. Kronick, a caring, skillful dentist in a small, isolated town. His patients love him for the time and concern he demonstrates toward each of them. Over time, his patients individually attempt to solicit his medical help with non-dental medical problems. One has serious flu-like symptoms, another has recurring back aches. His patients explain to him that the only MD in town, Dr. Olgavar, is gruff, arrogant, distant, and hopelessly out of date with modern medicine. Each extols Dr. Kronick's humanitarian virtues and pleads with him to help.

Dr. Kronick's position and your position are quite similar. You each are facing a real dilemma in the life of a person you care about and you want to help. If he gives non-dental medical advice or medical care, Dr. Kronick could lose his license to practice dentistry and be open to civil and criminal prosecution. Even more importantly, Dr. Kronick knows that he could do more harm than good for his desperate patients; he could actually compound his patient's problems by treating non-dental ailments. Recognizing that he is unqualified to provide care, he refers his patients to sources qualified and able to help: physicians other than Dr. Olgavar, the local branch of the American Medical Association, nearby health clinics, and so forth. Dr. Kronick knows that the best help he can give these patients is to refer them to the appropriate resources.

Make referrals. Your job is the same. The best and most caring course of action for you with Matthew is to refer him to the counseling center on your campus and, if available, other support groups on campus. You can empathize, "I'm really sorry this is happening to you," but you are not qualified to help and you could easily do more harm than good to try. A similar strategy applies to Maria, our anxious tutee from Situation #2.

Assess implications for today's tutoring. Incidentally, in cases like Matthew's and Maria's, where students are quite upset at a scheduled tutoring time, you will have to decide whether to continue with tutoring or whether to re-schedule. To make this decision, consider the tutee's wishes, the seriousness of the problem, and the degree to which the tutee seems preoccupied with the problem. Maria, for example, seems to become more agitated the more she discusses her problem, suggesting to Francisco that Maria is not ready to focus on the psychology class. Further, despite the fact that Francisco has expertise in the psychology course, he is not trained to help Maria cope with her feelings. Francisco can empathize with Maria's predicament but cannot embark on any intervention to help except to refer Maria to people and services trained to help with emotional upheaval.

Therefore, it is part of your function to be aware of the available services on your school campus and how to get in touch with them. At many campuses, such a directory exists. If not, encourage your supervisor to develop a list and make it available to tutors and students.

Notes:

EXERCISE: 1-1

You could further prepare yourself by reviewing the list of campus services, jotting down the types of problems students might have that are outside the scope of tutoring, and matching the types of problems with the available services. (i.e. debt, rape, health, etc.)

Services   Types of Problems

_____

_____

_____

_____

_____

_____

_____

_____

_____

_____

Notes:

THE GRAY AREA-BUT STILL OUT OF BOUNDS

Given that the tutoring role is focused on supporting instruction in specific classes or academic areas, you can see that attempting to provide assistance in areas such as serious debt, rape counseling, or complete parental rejection is clearly outside your role as a tutor. While less significant, roommate problems, transportation problems, and so forth are also clearly outside the scope of your tutoring role.

There are sets of problems, however, which are closer to your tutoring role but still inappropriate for you to take on. This section of the chapter intends to alert you to those problems and help you see why they fall outside the scope of your job as tutor. In doing so, I hope to further refine your sense of your role as a tutor. Examples of these types of problems include students who seek help outside of the usual process for receiving tutoring, teachers who ask you to substitute teach for them, and students who want you to do their work for them.

The six main goals of tutoring, discussed earlier in this chapter, are your mainstays in identifying requests or expectations which take you out of your role. Remember Situation 1: "Helpful" Paul expects Lisa to do some writing for him. Lisa goes against Tutoring Goals #1, #3, and #5 if she helps write Paul's paper. Goal #1 is to promote tutee independence. If Lisa does Paul's work, then he won't learn how to do it. His need for Lisa's help will intensify and so will the stridency of his requests for help. Goal #3 is to facilitate tutee insights. If Lisa does Paul's writing, Paul will not gain insights into *how* to develop his own writing nor will he learn more about the process. Goal #6 is follow the job description. I seriously doubt that any school requires its tutors to write for students, requires its tutors to make fun of students, or wants tutors to work in unsupervised settings. Knowing these goals and being able to apply them helps you stay focused on appropriate tasks and helps you recognize requests or expectations that take you out of your role.

HOW TO SAY NO

So now you know what you are expected to do and can recognize situations which can lead you out of your role. But what do you say to Paul, Maria, and Mr. Hoover, our antagonists from Situations #1, #2, and #3? How does one gracefully say no?

The first thing to realize is that saying "no" is more accurately described as saying "yes" to what you *can* do. If you say "no," you are more likely to enter into an escalating conflict in which you say you can't do some-

TUTOR ROLE

thing and the other pleads for you to do it. Saying what you can do as a tutor tends to pre-empt any conflict between another's inappropriate requests for help and your denials of the requests.

Francisco. So, Francisco can say to Maria, "That sounds really awful and I can see you're upset. I know where to find just the person for you to talk with." Francisco first acknowledges Maria's feelings (". . . sounds really awful. . . ") and, second, states what he can do ("I know where to find . . ."). This answers Maria's needs and keeps Francisco within his role as a tutor.

Kevin. What might Kevin say to Mr. Hoover? He has requested that he help him with various facets of his teaching and that he pretend it's tutoring. One of Kevin's possible responses is, "I'd love to help you with some of those things. My job is to tutor students. And, you know, I'm really looking forward to working with you about how to best tutor those students who need help with your class. But my job description specifically states that I can be paid by the tutoring center only for tutoring." As you can see, this is a sticky situation; one which Mr. Hoover can be faulted for creating. Even if Kevin completely partitions test correcting and substitute teaching from his tutoring responsibilities, the question remains whether it is wise or legal for him to substitute. What are the school policies regarding substitute qualifications and reimbursement? If he's not careful, Kevin could get himself into a very awkward spot.

If Mr. Hoover keeps the pressure on Kevin, even after he asserts his role as a tutor, then he may have to be more assertive. In this case, Kevin's strategy is to state *his* feelings of awkwardness, so that Mr. Hoover understands the spot in which he's putting him. Kevin could say, "You know, this is hard for me. I really admire you as a teacher and want to be a really good tutor. But these other requests put me in a bad spot." Kevin could then explain why he's in a bad spot and reiterate what he can do. In short, Kevin's strategy is to tell the truth about his feelings.

Lisa. The most complicated situation is Lisa's dilemma with the essay writing. Her situation is compounded by the fact that another tutor inappropriately helped Paul write his paper. Paul has come to regard this kind of help as usual and appropriate because another tutor has behaved as though it is. Each time Angela agreed to write for Paul, she legitimized the appropriateness of Paul's requests. Now, Lisa has two conflicting goals. First she has to indicate that Paul's requests have not been appropriate. Second, she has to indicate that doing Paul's work is inappropriate.

Saying what you can do as a tutor tends to pre-empt any conflict between another's inappropriate requests for help and your denials of the requests.

EXERCISE: 1-2

How could you apply what you learned from Francisco's and Kevin's situations to Lisa's situation? Imagine that you are the tutor trainer, that you are standing right behind Lisa when she responds to Paul, and that you can "freeze" time while you consult with Lisa. What would you tell Lisa?

_____

_____

_____

If you said assert what you can do as a tutor as opposed to what you can do as a writer, then you're on the right track. There's nothing wrong with saying, "No." You have every right to refuse to do anything which is outside your tutoring role or beyond your capabilities. When your statements of what you can do fail to solve a problem, then saying "no" is necessary and absolutely appropriate.

CONCLUSION

This text intends to help you get the most out of yourself and your tutoring sessions. This chapter sets the stage for conducting the day-to-day business of tutoring by helping you know what you are expected to do and why. Understanding the concept and goals of tutoring and communicating those clearly to others will enhance your enjoyment of and effectiveness with a most rewarding activity. Tutoring makes such a significant contribution to so many students, it's not sensible to waste your precious time and energy on activities which take you away from working with those students. Your tutoring sessions have the potential to provide you and your tutees with hundreds of small victories as you develop and refine skills for tutoring and as your students develop and refine skills for learning.

Notes:

CHAPTER 2:
THE TUTORING CYCLE

TUTORING
ROLE

**TUTORING
CYCLE**

TUTORING
OPTIONS

TUTORING
PATTERNS:

TUTORING
INTER-
CULTURALLY

23

CHAPTER 2: TUTORING CYCLE

Notes: ✍

INTRODUCTION

In Chapter 1: Tutoring Roles, you learned what a tutor is. In Chapter 2 the focus shifts to what a tutor *does*. The purpose of this chapter is to give you a sense of the typical steps to take in any tutoring session, to particularly emphasize steps which promote learning how to learn, and to give you some idea of how to initiate these steps in ways which respect the tutee's rightful quest for independence.

Remember the feeling you experienced when you first considered becoming a tutor? Most people in this situation first felt a swell of pride for being recruited and second felt a gulp of fear for what they'd gotten themselves into. Tutor? How do I do *that*? I don't know enough to stand up and lecture and even if I did, that doesn't seem like tutoring. HELP!

Fortunately, there is **The Tutoring Cycle:** a set of 12 steps which you can learn and then use to guide you through a tutoring session. Utilizing the steps in the tutoring cycle will help you tutor effectively and efficiently and will help the tutee be a more independent learner. *In this chapter you will learn about the 12 Steps of The Tutoring Cycle, understand the reasons for taking each step, and practice knowing what to say to begin each step.*

The word cycle is important because learning is, in a way, cyclical. In general terms, one first identifies what is to be learned, consciously or unconsciously sets some strategy for learning, learns, then moves on to the next learning task; and the cycle continues. The Tutor Cycle provides more detailed structure as to how one learns and specifically adapts the structure to a tutoring encounter. The Tutoring Cycle is diagrammed in Figure 2-1 on page 25. Let's review each of the steps below.

THE 12 STEPS OF THE TUTOR CYCLE		
BEGINNING STEPS	**TASK STEPS**	**CLOSING STEPS**
STEP 1 Greeting and Climate Setting	STEP 5 Set the Agenda For The Session	STEP 9 Confirmation
STEP 2 Identification of Task	STEP 6 Addressing the Task	STEP 10 What Next?
STEP 3 Breaking the Task Into Parts	STEP 7 Tutee Summary of Content	STEP 11: Arranging and Planning the Next Session
STEP 4 Identification of Thought Processes Which Underlie Task	STEP 8 Tutee Summary of Underlying Process	STEP 12 Closing and Good-bye

Figure 2-1

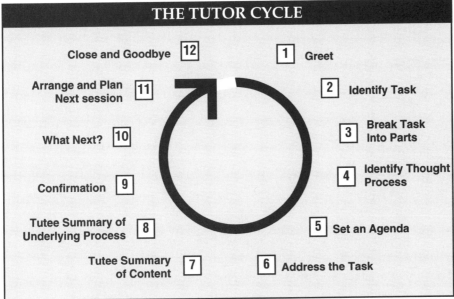

THE TUTOR CYCLE

Close and Goodbye [12] [1] Greet

Arrange and Plan [11] [2] Identify Task
Next session

What Next? [10] [3] Break Task Into Parts

Confirmation [9] [4] Identify Thought Process

Tutee Summary of [8] [5] Set an Agenda
Underlying Process

Tutee Summary [7] [6] Address the Task
of Content

STEPS OF THE TUTORING CYCLE

STEP 1: GREETING AND CLIMATE SETTING

The overall purpose of Step 1 of the Tutor Cycle is to set up the session for success. Any time two or more people meet, each first greets the other. We all recognize these greetings: a "hello" or a "hi" or "hey, how's it goin'?" In a tutoring situation this greeting is accompanied by setting a positive tone for the session. The warmth of the greeting, the arrangement of chairs and tables to facilitate interaction, eye contact, and smiles are each related to a positive tone. The arrangement of the furniture may seem petty, but it is important. Many tutors are reluctant to move furniture even when it is necessary.

Recall a few times in your own classes when you were asked to form small groups. How did people arrange their seating? Even though we all know that a perfect circle gives every person equal opportunity to participate as a talker and a listener, we didn't usually form good circles. As is shown in Figure 2-2, when the circle is poorly formed, some students have to turn in awkward positions to see others, some can't hear others, and so forth. As a result, some students have an easier time being a part of the group than do others. In Figure 2-2, all students have equal access to each other in Circle #2. In Circle #1, D is at a disadvantage because he is so far removed from A and B.

Notes: ✍

Figure 2-2
A comparison of two groups of students

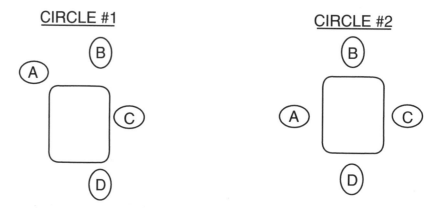

In your tutoring sessions be proactive: take positive steps to ensure the most productive seating. If you are working with a group arrange a good circle. Have only the chairs you need and eliminate vacant spaces. To accommodate a late comer, widen the circle's diameter, rather than letting the latecomer sit on the fringe of the circle.

If you are involved in one to one tutoring, sit side by side with the work in front of the student or between you. Allow for whether the student is right or left-handed. Sit to the right of a right hander, to the left for a left hander. This will put you closest to the work and, if you are right handed, less able to write on it.

Please remember to keep your hands off the student's work. If pages need to be turned, let the tutee do it. If there is something to be written, let the tutee do it. Whatever tools you're using — pencil, pen, chalk, chalkboard — should be in the hands of the tutee. Remember, your goal is to promote the tutee's independence.

STEP 2: IDENTIFICATION OF TASK

Once you have greeted each other and arranged the seating, the next step is to figure out the purpose of the tutoring session. What is it the tutee wishes to work on? If given the opportunity, nearly all tutees will voluntarily state what it is they wish to work on. Therefore, you can best help tutees by giving them the opportunity to indicate what they would like help with.

Provide opportunity. Eager tutors often don't give their tutees the opportunity. A tutor who acts for the tutee, and before the tutee, puts the tutee behind. Your tutee knows she is seeing you for help. Let her direct your attention to her needs on her terms and at her pace. This keeps her in charge of her learning and provides her the opportunity to act as a peer with you. She directs your attention rather than the other way around.

Notes:

If it becomes clear that the tutee is avoiding getting down to business, then you can say something like, "How is that math class going?" Such a statement focuses the discussion but is not as directive as, "*Tell me* what you need to work on today."

Some of your tutees will likely be more specific and more clear on the day's focus than will other of your tutees. The tutee who is clearer may say, "I don't understand how to develop good transitions in this essay." One who feels more lost may say, "I need help with my writing." Assume that those who are less focused need to learn more about how to focus their questions and to feel less overwhelmed. Do not assume that they are somehow deficient. You are in a position to help with effective follow-up questions or statements.

Follow up. Your follow-up questions or statements can accomplish two objectives at once. First, your follow up can help tutees make statements which clarify their immediate concerns. Second, your follow up can reinforce the fact that your tutees do know something and that it is on their knowledge that you intend to build. Building on tutees' knowledge is a healthier approach to learning because it respects and acknowledges what the tutee has learned and does know. Reinforcing the tutee as a knowledgeable person empowers the tutee.

Restatements. To this end, give the tutee the opportunity to acknowledge for herself what she knows and to focus the day's activities. If the tutee states, "I need help with my writing," then you can simply repeat her statement, "You need help with your writing." Then pause. The tutee will likely clarify in some way, "Yeah, I got this essay and the teacher said something about transitions." Now you're on your way. The session is developing a focus and the tutee is doing the focusing. As you will learn in Chapter 3, your best way to help, surprisingly, is the pause!

Empathetic statement. In addition to restatements, another strategy is to offer an empathetic statement. "Writing a good paper for Mr. Periwinkleton can be really frustrating." These kinds of statements promote the tutee's independence by giving her the opportunity to define the topic of tutoring.

Before proceeding to the next step in The Tutoring Cycle be sure you understand what the tutee needs help with. It may take more time at the beginning of a session, but it will definitely save time later in the session.

Notes: ✐

You're much better off spending one or two minutes now on clearly identifying the topic than spending ten or fifteen minutes later tutoring something the tutee doesn't need help with.

STEP 3: BREAKING THE TASK INTO PARTS

Because most tasks that tutees define for tutoring have several parts or a sequence of parts, you and the tutee will have to work out the sequence and duration of each part. Let's recall the empowerment and independence goals. Again, more skillful tutors behave in ways which permit the tutee the opportunity to break the task into parts. Let's return to the example of the student needing help with transitions in an essay. Possible steps include knowing what a transition is, knowing where they go, identifying places in her essay where transitions are needed, and writing transitions for each of those places.

<u>Providing opportunity.</u> How can you behave in ways that give the tutee the opportunity to carry out this step? Here again, a restatement is a useful technique. If Julia, your tutee, says, "I've got to understand mitosis, be able to diagram it, identify each of the parts in each of the stages . . . Boy!" you could restate what she just said only more calmly, "Boy, that is a lot! Let's see, understand mitosis, diagram it, label the parts." Julia has the opportunity to say, "Do you think we can do that in the time we have?" You could say, "What are those three things again you want to do?" This approach reinforces that there are three distinct tasks and suggests that there is a sequence to them. Remember also that a pause — doing nothing but continuing to listen — will often lead to the tutee providing more information.

STEP 4: IDENTIFICATION OF THOUGHT PROCESSES WHICH UNDERLIE THE TASK

This is one of two of the most critical steps in tutoring. Unfortunately, the two most critical steps in The Tutoring Cycle are also the least practiced. Step #4 is one, #8 is the other. Unless you make a concerted effort to do these steps, it won't happen. After reading this paragraph, you probably have the idea that I am emphasizing their importance! You're right!

Step 4: Identifying the underlying thought processes means that you help the tutee learn how to approach learning the type of task with which he is having problems.

The type of task is determined by the particular focus of your individual tutoring session. Let's look at an example.

Unfortunately, the two most critical steps in The Tutoring Cycle are also the least practiced. Step #4 is one, #8 is the other.

Suppose you're a math tutor and you have agreed to work with Damien, the tutee, on solving an equation with one variable. The first problem might be something like,

1.) $15 - 3x + 12 = 5x - 3 + 2x$

What is the process underlying this task? The basic process is to get all the variables (-3x, 5x, and 2x) on one side of the equation and all the numbers (14, 12, and -3) on the other side and then do the mathematical operations necessary to reduce the numbers to one number on one side of the equation and reducing the variables to an unencumbered "x" on the other side. Reducing the equation is accomplished by adding, subtracting, multiplying or dividing numbers or variables from both sides of the equation. So, for example, one might eliminate the "-3x" from the left side by adding "3x" to each side. Ultimately, the problem is solved when the equation is reduced to an equation such as "x = 3". But is Damien's problem solved? NO!

If not trained otherwise, the vast majority of tutors would do this problem for Damien and *not talk about a general approach for doing this type of problem*. Your task is to help Damien become independent. Thus, showing Damien how to do this *type* of problem using this *particular* problem as the example helps him develop skills for operating independently of you. However, if the exclusive focus of your tutoring session is what answer goes on the line on his answer sheet, then you're answering Damien's immediate need. However, answering his immediate need doesn't give him much help for knowing how to work out what goes on the next blank line.

Promoting independence. How should you help Damien? First ask him to explain to you how he'll proceed with each of the problems in the assigned problem set. Your objective is to hear a fairly detailed procedure. Once a procedure has been articulated, say something like, "Why don't you apply those steps to the first problem?" This way you're encouraging the student to develop a learning strategy for doing problems of this type and to practice applying that learning strategy. His experiences utilizing the learning strategy will make him more comfortable with the idea of using learning strategies and lead to refinements and modifications. Goals of independence and empowerment are achieved because Damien develops and uses tools for learning which can continue to be used when he's studying by himself.

Information sources. Throughout the process of helping a student develop skills for doing problems of this type, keep in mind that the course materials — textbook, handouts, workbooks, lecture notes, etc. — are the source of information. You, the tutor, are not the source of information, these

Showing Damien how to do this type of problem . . . . . helps him develop skills for operating independently of you.

. . . course materials . . . are the source of information. You, the tutor, are not the source of information . . .

Notes:

Notes: ✍

You don't want to become the one who processes course information and then explains it to the student . . . . . preventing the tutee from being able to do the processing themselves.

materials are. You don't want to become the one who processes course information and then explains it to the student. You want the student to process information in the course materials for himself. If you always explain the information to the student, then how will the student learn how to get information from course materials?

Many tutors, out of the best of intentions, explain course materials to their tutees, ironically preventing the tutee from being able to do the processing themselves. Thus, these tutors' best intentions actually increase tutees' dependence on them. Take a look at your textbooks and other course materials. How important is it to your success as a student that you know *how* to use these materials for your own learning?

Let's go back to you and Damien. If he doesn't understand how to reduce the equation, then where is the information which can help him? Many math texts are organized in basically the same way. There is probably a chapter on solving simple equations. This chapter first identifies the concept, in this case, "Solving Simple Equations." The first part of the chapter likely offers a definition — an explanation of what a simple equation is and perhaps a brief rationale explaining the importance of knowing how to solve them. The explanation probably makes connections with what was covered in the previous chapter. Then, the authors of the text probably walk the reader through each step of an example problem. Then there is a sample problem in which the steps to the solution are eliminated but the answer is given. Following that you may find a problem set in which the problems progress from easier to harder. Sound familiar? This is the information Damien needs.

You can direct Damien's attention to the text by saying, "Let's see how the text tells you how to do these kinds of problems." Or you could say, "I know the explanation in the text helped me when I took the class." Or, "Good thing for you and me Ms. Sharp picked a text with a good explanation of how to do this stuff." In each case you are showing the tutee that the information he needs is available to him as a result of efforts he makes. It's not your job to explain the information to him, but to help him get it for himself.

At this point you may be thinking, "But I tutor English or foreign language or physics or aeronautical bird tracking." The same tutoring strategy applies. What is the process for doing this type of task and where is this process explained? Consider once again the description of the typical math chapter in the previous paragraph. In an English grammar class, for example, the same basic format may well apply. First a concept is introduced and given a label — pronoun agreement, for example. Then the concept is defined and its usefulness explained. Then there are sample problems followed by a problem

TUTORING CYCLE

set. In the problem set, students identify pronouns and figure out how to make sure the correct pronouns are used. Physics students may also recognize the basic structure. Imagine a chapter on levers. It's likely that in the chapter there are exercises in which students calculate energy needed to move a weight using a lever with a fulcrum. The aeronautical bird tracking thing? Lemme get back to you on that.

Notes: ✎

<u>Utilize the text</u>. Again take a look at the materials your students have available to them. How is the information organized? What are the steps to understanding and applying this information? If your tutees don't learn how to learn from their course materials, then they will always need someone else to explain it. Not much independence there. If the students are able to learn from their text and can figure out how to apply it, then they have a skill useful to them for a lifetime.

Make sure that in your tutoring sessions, your tutee talks about how to do the type of task that he wants help with. Remember that whatever particular task he wants help with is just one example of a collection of similar tasks. More than any other step in The Tutoring Cycle, Step 4: Identification of Thought Processes Which Underlie the Task, is critical to your tutee's development as an independent and empowered learner. The first four steps (i.e. Beginning Steps) are reviewed below.

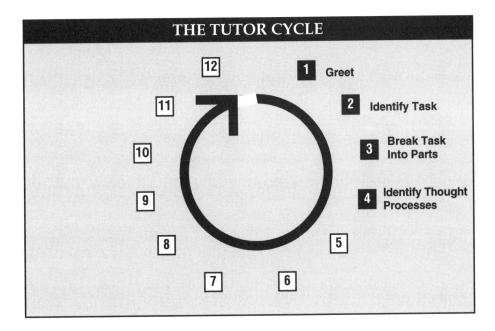

THE TUTOR CYCLE

1 Greet
2 Identify Task
3 Break Task Into Parts
4 Identify Thought Processes

STEP 5: SET AN AGENDA FOR THE SESSION

The efficient accomplishment of any task involves first knowing what the task is and secondly allocating available time to the task. An agenda is a plan allocating time to a task. It's like a budget for time. How much time do we have and how shall we spend it? In any given tutoring session, how much time do you have and how will you spend it?

Again, remember a tutor's tendency may be to take the initiative in beginning each step of The Tutoring Cycle. However, more effective tutors find ways to get the tutee actively involved in initiating each step. When setting the agenda, these skillful tutors use statements such as, "Well, we have 40 minutes, how shall we use them?" or "How shall we allocate the time we have remaining?" These kinds of statements make sure that the tutee has a hand in shaping the agenda. Giving the tutee the opportunity to set the agenda greatly increases the likelihood that the tutee will actively participate in making the agenda work.

<u>Follow the agenda but be flexible.</u> Once set, an agenda is a plan which you should make every effort to follow. If it is too vague or too easily ignored, then you're accidentally teaching the tutee that the agenda is something you set and ignore. Further, a tutee won't learn how to accurately budget time if time is haphazardly spent. Correspondingly, sticking slavishly to an agenda in light of an overwhelming need to reallocate time is equally nonproductive. Your goal is to help the tutee accurately assess the amount of time needed to complete the identified learning tasks. If it's obvious that the time allocation is off, then readjust.

It's important that the agenda be explicitly stated. If both you and the tutee have a hand in creating it, then you will both have a hand in making it work. Making the agenda explicit helps the student have an active role in deciding what to learn and planning adequate time to learn it.

STEP 6: ADDRESSING THE TASK

Once you have established the tone for the session, identified a task, identified the underlying thought processes for the task, and set the agenda, then you commence the next step of tutoring. In this step of The Tutoring Cycle you and the tutee follow your learning agenda and conduct the business of tutoring. The information in the next chapter, Tutoring Decisions: Moves and Strategies is particularly directed to this step. Once again, keep in mind that the source of information is the course materials not your understanding of them. Help the tutee learn from the materials.

STEP 7: TUTEE SUMMARY OF CONTENT

This step of the Tutoring Cycle is where you see results. Your tutee demonstrates what she has learned often in a spontaneous burst of excitement. When she sees the light, you will know it. Your biology tutee, Helena, will say something to the effect of, "Oh, I get it! Red blood cells are important for health because . . ." Or, your English tutee, Diego, may say, "Oh, OK! A metaphor is just like a simile except that . . ." You might call this important moment in tutoring **"The Light Bulb Effect"** because Helena's and Diego's faces light up and their talk becomes animated. They may well have interrupted your talk to share their excitement.

Note also that in each of their quotes, Helena and Diego are beginning to explain what they have learned. When you see and hear this explanation, Step 7 is happening. For you, it's rather like being there when a baby is being born. It's going to happen no matter what you do, so you better just help without getting in the way!

Stay out of the way. And get out of the way is just the appropriate tack for a skillful tutor to take. Explaining what one has just learned is more than just unabated excitement; it is an important component of learning. When Diego explains what he has just learned about metaphors and similes, the process of explaining helps move that information from short term memory to long term memory.

Short and long term memory. Say what? Short term memory? Long term memory? **Short term memory** is what you do when you remember items to buy at the grocery store as you walk in; it's what a waiter does when he remembers who ordered what at a given table. It's called short term because it is just that — the place where bits of information are held in memory for a short period of time. For many pieces of information short term memory is all you want. You have no need to remember your grocery list from six months ago. A waiter doesn't need to remember who ordered the extra rutabaga once it is delivered to your table. All new information is first

Notes:

placed in our short term memory. We have to do something to emphasize it in order to place it into our long term memory. Short term memory is like information you type on a computer screen. Long term memory places that information in a file and can retrieve it.

Long term memory is also what its name states: the place where you put information you will need to be able to retrieve later. For example, if you're married, you are wise to place the date of your wedding in long term memory. Conjugating verbs in a second language, factoring equations, the route from your house to the post office, economic causes of the War Between the States, how to use *The Reader's Guide to Periodical Literature*, and if you're really brave, how to program your VCR are all examples of information placed into long term memory.

Provide opportunity. Back to the light bulb effect. Your tutee, Odell, has just excitedly proclaimed, "Oh, I get it! Freud's theory of personality . . ." What is your strategy at this point? If you said, "Well I'm excited too so I'll help him explain," then see if the rutabaga-serving waiter needs an assistant. If you said, "Let his explanation run its course without interrupting it," then put the rutabaga on the back burner, your career as a tutor just got more secure. His explanation helps him move the information from short term memory to long term memory.

Odell's explanation also helps both of you evaluate the accuracy and completeness of his understanding. Pay close attention to Odell's explanation as it will reveal to you what he understands. But do not interrupt him to correct a mis-statement or a gap. Let him continue and you will then give him the opportunity to correct himself or indicate for himself areas in which he is unsure. Once the tutee takes over the explanation, many skilled tutors say no more than "Right," or "Yes," or "Uh huh," until their tutees direct a question to them *and* their tutees pause for a significant period of time after the question. Given these two events, a question and a significant pause, these tutors then figure that their tutees' explanations have run their course and that it's appropriate for the tutor to say something.

The fake "light bulb." But what happens if the tutee says he understands why Freud is important to the early study of personality, but doesn't offer any explanation. Odell says, "Oh OK, I get it. Thanks." Think carefully; you don't want to serve rutabaga. This may be the "fake light bulb effect." In this case the tutee believes this is the point where he should have gotten it, but hasn't. He is embarrassed for not getting it and doesn't want to appear

34   TUTORING CYCLE

stupid. Your job is to keep the session at this step of the cycle or to back track in the cycle until the tutee can explain the information. What you accomplish in a tutoring session is a product of the efforts of both the tutor and the tutee.

After Odell says, "Oh OK, I get it. Thanks," give him plenty of time to keep talking. You do this by saying nothing. After you say nothing, he may say something like, "But I guess I'm still a little unclear about what the difference is between id, ego, and superego." Then you return to Step 6 of The Tutoring Cycle. If after Odell says, "Oh OK, I get it. Thanks," he says nothing else, then your task is to find out what he does understand and what he is less clear about. You can say something like, "Let's just review Freud's theory for a minute." This gives him the opportunity to explain — maybe he really does understand. If he doesn't explain, it gives him the opportunity to indicate that some more review may help. "Maybe it would be good to look at that section of the book again."

Overall then, Step 7: Tutee Summary of the Content helps the tutee move information from short term to long term memory and helps both you and the tutee evaluate the depth and breadth of the tutee's understanding. In many cases, this step occurs spontaneously. In other cases, especially when the tutee doesn't understand, your objective is to make sure this step happens.

STEP 8: TUTEE SUMMARY OF UNDERLYING PROCESS

Step 8 is the companion to Step 4 which first introduced you to the thought processes underlying the tutee's task. This is the second of the two most important steps. Where Step 4 identified the underlying process, Step 8 reinforces it by having the tutee summarize the process as he understands it.

You may recall that in Step 4, your objective was to identify the thinking processes that underlie the type of task your tutee needs to work on. Helping your tutee learn the underlying processes helps him develop skills for doing similar tasks independently. You probably also recall that unless you consciously act otherwise, your tutee won't work on these underlying thinking skills at all. Thus, Step 8 occurs even less often than Step 4, because the appearance of Step 8 is dependent on the appearance of Step 4.

Your task in Step 8 is to be sure that a summary statement of the learning process happens. In your early tutoring sessions with a given tutee, you will most likely have to intervene to make sure that this step happens. For help on how to intervene, we can draw from Step 7 because that step promotes a tutee summary just as this one does.

Helping your tutee learn the underlying processes helps him develop skills for doing similar tasks independently . . . . . Your task in Step 8 is to be sure that a summary statement of the learning process happens.

Notes: ✎

In Step 7, when the tutee didn't summarize the content, then you tried to give him the opportunity to do so. In Step 8, you behave in a similar manner to get your tutee to explain *how* to do the type of task on which you're focused. To initiate this step, you might say something like, "Suppose a friend of yours asked you how to do these problems. What would you say?" Or you might say to your tutee, "That's great that you worked out the answer. How'd you do it?" Or, "Suppose you encounter a similar problem on the test. How will you solve it?"

Provide opportunity. Your objective is to cause the tutee to explain the thought processes he/she used, knowing that such an explanation helps move the understanding from short term to long term memory and also helps you and the tutee assess understanding. Further, keep in mind that unless you act to make this step happen, it probably won't. However, if in each session with each of your tutees, you consistently include this step, then your tutees will come to anticipate it and will help make it happen. Thus, your longer range objective is to behave in ways which helps the tutee internalize the steps of The Tutoring Cycle so that it is the tutee who initiates each step.

The second four steps (i.e. Task Steps) are reviewed below.

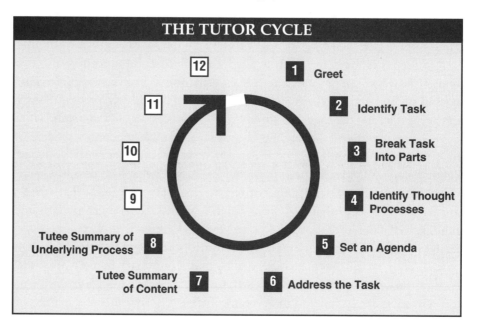

Step 9: Confirmation

Once the tutee has explained the content and the process (Steps 7 and 8), then you already know what to do. Tutors almost universally offer some kind of congratulatory statement confirming that their tutees do in fact understand. These statements are usually simple and direct, "Good job!" or "That sounds right to me," or "Good!" All of these statements serve the same function: they let the tutee know that what he/she has learned is accurate and appropriate.

<u>Reinforce specific accomplishments</u>. More skillful tutors tie the confirmation to specific statements or accomplishments. Thus, "Good job!" becomes "You did a skillful job of factoring that equation, particularly when you immediately got all the variables on the same side of the equals sign." Or, "I wish you'd been my friend when I took that class. I definitely could have used your explanation of how to do that kind of problem! You particularly cleared up the important difference between a metaphor and a simile." Reinforcing specific behaviors helps the tutee know what to keep doing.

<u>Thoughtful evaluations</u>. Evaluating another, whether praising, encouraging, or pointing out weaknesses, calls for some thoughtfulness on your part. *Evaluating is like perfume; a little goes a long way and it's best to apply it in key spots.* Too much praise and a person receiving it can become overwhelmed by it. Imagine the scene in a department store where a person is offering samples of a new perfume. A shopper might be grateful for a well-placed dab of perfume but would be offended by having it loaded on, "Do I smell so bad I need this much perfume?" Similarly a tutee lavished with too much praise might wonder, "Do I seem so weak I need this much encouragement?"

An additional and important concern surrounding evaluating another is that, by definition, *an evaluator occupies a power position* in relation to the one being evaluated. For the moment anyway, the evaluator is a judge and the person being evaluated the defendant. Perhaps right now you could think for a minute about how you might offer encouragement to another which doesn't over-kill and also respects the other's independence. What might you say?

More successful tutors tend to tie praise to specific parts of a student's work, thus separating the value of the work from the value of the person producing it. Tutors also encourage tutees to evaluate themselves or to be proud of their own work so that the evaluation is internalized. The tutee is encouraged to look inward as a result and not to you for approval and a sense

Notes: ✍

of well being. You might say something such as, "You've worked really hard for that answer," followed by a pause in which the tutee can agree *and* elaborate.

Similarly, any negative evaluations should be directed to the student's work or to the two of you, tutor and tutee, as a unit. "We've really strayed away from our plan for the day" is much easier to hear and probably more accurate than, "You're really off track right now." Where the first statement is an *observation* about the tutor *and* the tutee, the second assigns *responsibility* exclusively to the tutee. Generally, if the tutoring session winds up in a place a tutor thinks is not productive, the tutor has had a hand in creating that situation. Observing that the *two of you together* have drifted off track takes the onus off the tutee and focuses concern on what to do about it, not on who's at fault.

STEP 10: WHAT NEXT?

Having confirmed your tutee's understanding, you can then help the tutee anticipate what she will do next. This not only helps her plan what she could do next, it also reinforces connections between what she learned in tutoring and what she'll be learning next. Helping your tutee anticipate what's next helps her see that the bits of knowledge she picks up in class, in tutoring, and studying on her own are actually connected. It helps her apply and build on what she learned in tutoring. You might say something such as, "Well, where do you go from here in this class?" or "What will you do next and how will what we've done help you?"

STEP 11: ARRANGING AND PLANNING THE NEXT SESSION

Arranging and planning the next session involves both setting a time and place to next meet (usually handled by an appointment procedure) and anticipating what kinds of tasks the tutee may wish to address. The main benefits of this step of The Tutoring Cycle are: (a) it takes care of scheduling the next appointment while the student is in the place where appointments are made; (b) it promotes some consistency in tutoring and thus maximizes student gains; and (c) it helps the tutee anticipate upcoming learning.

The stair syndrome. Have you ever heard of the stair syndrome? Probably not, as I just made it up. Anyway, the stair syndrome holds that the more stairs or the farther across campus a student must walk to seek out a non-mandatory service, the less likely he is to seek out that service. Whether your tutoring is appointment-based or drop in, you can help your tutee avoid the stair syndrome. If your tutoring results from appointments, have the student sign up for a new appointment on the way out the door. If your tutoring is drop in, then you can at least indicate to the student the times you are next available for drop in. Scheduling in advance helps the student feel more welcome in your tutoring center and helps him plan to get the help he needs. If your tutoring is scheduled for the term (certain students come each week at a specified time), then you don't have to worry about scheduling, but you *can* plan.

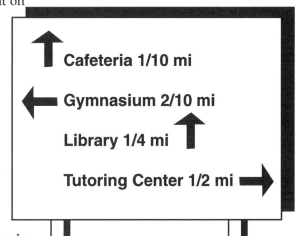

Planning involves spending a moment or two talking about what you and the tutee might do in the next session. Thus for example, if today your tutoring session with Rafael focused on developing a topic for an analytical essay assignment in his English 1A class, then next week's session might involve looking at the logic of his analysis. Planning in this way helps Rafael set and keep a schedule for completing his assignment. He knows that in order to review the logic of his paper he has to have a draft of the paper prepared. Planning also helps you each know where to begin each session.

<u>Providing opportunity</u>. Here, as in other steps of The Tutoring Cycle, your task is to behave in ways which give the student the opportunity to carry out this step. As always, if you ask an open-ended question, you give Rafael more freedom in how he answers. An outcome of his freedom is that it reinforces his independence from you. He isn't following your commands or doing what you request, he is deciding for himself. Think about what you might say to initiate this step. "Shall we meet again?" is much more open than, "You need to see me at this time next week." Similarly, "What would you like to work on next week?" is more open than "Next week we'll review your paper for adequate support." The key here is that the tutee makes the decision not you. You're just bringing the idea up for consideration.

<u>Encouraging dependence</u>. At first thought you may think that encouraging the student to come back for more tutoring promotes dependence not independence. A basic irony is definitely operating here: more

tutoring for Rafael will help him get to a place where he won't need more tutoring. His contact with you is helping him learn how to function effectively for himself so that he doesn't need to be tutored.

Of course, it may be that Rafael doesn't need to come back next week; that he's ready to do his work independently. If that's the case, then obviously you won't be helping him by insisting that he come back anyway. When you get to the point where a student may not need to come back, then briefly discuss this with him. Your relationship of trust and regard exists whether he comes back or not.

STEP 12: CLOSING AND GOOD-BYE

The last step in The Tutoring Cycle will occur without any training. Just as the social convention of greeting each other is strong, so is the convention of saying good-bye. It only takes a couple of seconds so make it a sincere good-bye. Many tutees will thank you for your help. You might thank the tutee for some specific contribution she made, "Thanks for being so prepared," or "Thanks for taking the time to explain the assignment so well to me." The objective, of course, is to leave on a positive note. This completes the 12 steps in the Tutoring Cycle as the diagram below shows.

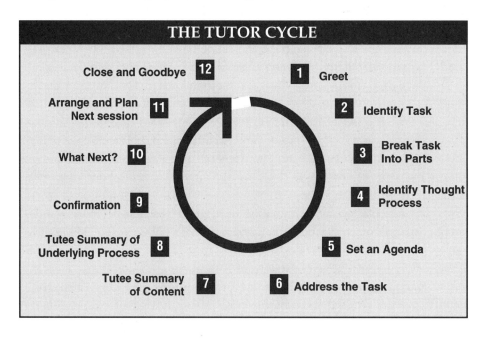

THE TUTOR CYCLE

Close and Goodbye **12**
Arrange and Plan Next session **11**
What Next? **10**
Confirmation **9**
Tutee Summary of Underlying Process **8**
Tutee Summary of Content **7**

1 Greet
2 Identify Task
3 Break Task Into Parts
4 Identify Thought Process
5 Set an Agenda
6 Address the Task

TUTORING CYCLE

BENEFITS OF THE CYCLE

Notes:

Taken together, the 12 Steps of The Tutoring Cycle have several bene-fits. First, they help you move most efficiently and effectively through a tutor-ing session. Second, understanding and following these steps demystifies the tutoring process. What does one do when one tutors? One follows these steps and behaves in ways which promote the tutee's internalization of them. Third, the steps reinforce to the tutee a practical approach to learning, by emphasizing learning how to learn. Fourth, the 12 Steps of the Tutoring Cycle are relatively easy to follow. Many, such as saying hello and good-bye, will occur naturally because they are social conventions inculcated in us from our social experiences. Ironically those steps that don't occur naturally are the most important. They have been emphasized in the discussion. Of these, Step 4 and Step 8 are most critical, as they emphasize the thinking processes which are needed to do the type of task with which the student has difficulty.

"Not enough time!" Many tutors' first reaction to learning these steps is some version of, "If I took the time to do all 12 steps there wouldn't be any time left for tutoring!" This reaction is understandable but inaccurate. I think you'll see the inaccuracy of this assumption by completing the following exercise.

EXERCISE: 2-1

Consider the first three steps of The Tutoring Cycle: 1) greet; 2) identify task; 3) break into parts. Write down what you might say to initiate each of these steps. Then get together with another tutor. Read each statement you've written while your partner times in seconds how long each state-ment takes.

Statement   Time

_____

_____

_____

_____

_____

_____

TUTORING CYCLE

Most likely each statement takes less than ten seconds to say out loud. Our assumptions about dialog may be more derived from movies, TV, and novels, than from our own experiences. In real life, we just talk to each other; only a few study the dynamics of the talk itself. Dialog in real life moves somewhat faster than what is characterized in TV or movies, and written dialog seems as though it will take significantly longer to say than it really does. If you are still not convinced that carrying out these steps takes less time than you think, observe a session by an experienced and skilled tutor who actually utilizes The Tutoring Cycle. How long do any of the first three or four steps take?

If you are *still* unconvinced, consider helping the waiter deliver extra helpings of rutabaga. Just kidding. Think of the consequences of omitting some of the steps in The Tutoring Cycle. Any one you eliminate can lead to time consuming problems later in the session. You see no need to set an agenda, for example? Imagine the time it creates to straighten out the confusion that can result when you and your tutee are at cross purposes about *what* you will do *when*. You see no need to spend time figuring out what the day's task is?

Imagine a doctor who just prescribes some medicine on guesswork because running valid tests and taking a patient history takes a lot of time. How can the doctor know what to prescribe without first knowing what the patient's concerns are? In the same way, you as a tutor can not really just tutor without first knowing what your tutee's concerns are. Just doing something may be efficient in the short term, but is quite inefficient in the long run. Just as the doctor's patient will keep seeking help for the same unidentified ailment until it is correctly diagnosed, so will a tutee continue to need assistance until his concerns are accurately identified.

CONCLUSION

Each step in the cycle is necessary. Omitting one to save time is false economy and deprives the student of opportunities to make the most out of his/her time with you. If you follow the steps of the Cycle, you will find that your tutees will quickly learn to initiate more and more of the steps on their own. As they take more initiative, they are demonstrating exactly the kind of independence you want and are also internalizing a process for productive and efficient learning. Requiring particular effort are Steps #4 and #8: identifying thought processes and tutee summary of underlying process. They are critical for the development of independent learning skills and so require your extra effort to make them happen. In the next chapter you will learn more about your communication options in tutoring and how to select among them most effectively.

Steps #4 and #8: . . . . . are critical for the development of independent learning skills and so require your extra effort . . . . .

TUTORING CYCLE

CHAPTER 3:
TUTORING OPTIONS

TUTORING
ROLE

TUTORING
CYCLE

**TUTORING
OPTIONS**

TUTORING
PATTERNS:

TUTORING
INTER-
CULTURALLY

CHAPTER 3: TUTORING OPTIONS

Active listening is an art . . . . . tutors who can adapt their listening and talk behaviors to the specifics of a tutoring situation are more likely to be successful.

INTRODUCTION

Active listening is an art; it is at the core of tutoring. An effective tutor learns a balance between talk and quiet. Talk alone is not enough. While anyone can *tell* a person what to think or do, real learning takes place within the individual in the quiet moments between words. Listening and quiet play a large part in this equation. Human beings are characteristically thoughtful creatures. We need the freedom to think about an idea before we capture it as our own. You may wonder how this is possible in a tutorial setting. We will examine this idea as the chapter unfolds.

On a moment-to-moment basis in tutoring, you will be making countless decisions about when to talk and when to listen. When you talk, you will be deciding what to say to your tutee. In this chapter, you will learn how to form your decisions about *how you listen and talk* with your tutees. Think ahead about these decisions by learning about your options. It better prepares you to make these decisions seamlessly and effectively.

Considerable evidence suggests that the best teachers — and therefore tutors as well — have developed what might be called **linguistic flexibility: a set of abilities related to thinking constructively about what they say; quickly developing alternative ways of expressing ideas; and incorporating into their own speech ideas, words, and phrases introduced by their students.** Being linguistically flexible means that teachers can quickly account for the demands of specific situations with specific students, generate options for communicating successively, and enact more suitable options. Linguistic flexibility also knows the value of quiet, and when it is appropriate. Similarly, *tutors who can adapt their listening and talk behaviors to the specifics of a tutoring situation are more likely to be successful.*

PURPOSE AND ORGANIZATION OF THIS CHAPTER

The purpose of this chapter is to help you develop flexibility by presenting the basic components of tutoring talk. There are six kinds of techniques for tutoring talk: **initiate, reply, evaluate, explain, active listening, and quiet**. Each is an option for you to use at any given moment in your tutoring.

The chapter is divided into six sections, one for each option. Also in each section, there is a focused discussion of how to enact each option most effectively in your tutoring. Sample dialogs and tutoring situations will illustrate each option and give you practice in applying what you learn.

OVERVIEW OF OPTIONS

Remember our discussion of short term memory in Chapter 2? The portion of your thinking which displays information for immediate use? In this chapter, you are being asked to place some information about tutoring in your short-term memory and use that information while you tutor. People who study human memory tell us that humans can hold six or seven pieces of information in memory while they carry out some task related to those bits of information. If people are required to remember more than that, they are much more likely to experience difficulty with remembering those bits of information or with carrying out the task. Therefore, options for tutoring talk have been reduced to six, ensuring that you can be engaged in tutoring effectively while still keeping these options in mind.

I can hear you speaking to me now. "You're telling me every time it's my turn at talk, I am expected to stop tutoring while I analyze the situation, survey my options, figure out which option is most appropriate, and then formulate a statement which enacts that option? When am I supposed to tutor?" You're right. You can't be this deliberate about every move in your tutoring. What you can do is be aware of the six options and utilize this understanding to influence your own behavior.

Just what are options for talk? **An option is either (a) any statement a tutor or tutee makes which has a particular intent — to ask a question, give an answer, etc., or (b) doing nothing so the other will do something.** As stated earlier, there are six options: initiate, reply, evaluate, explain, active listening, and quiet.

DIFFERENCES BETWEEN OPTION AND TURN AT TALK

Please keep in mind that there is a difference between an option and a turn at talk. A turn at talk occurs when one person talks, without interruption, until another speaks. A turn at talk may be one word or several paragraphs. It starts when one starts speaking and ends when another starts speaking. In the following dialog there are three turns at talk. Note that each turn begins when the person starts talking and ends when the next person starts talking. (The superscripted "T" identifies the tutor.)

turn at talk #1 — · ➤	H^T: So you've been working on your essay.
turn at talk #2 — · ➤	D: Yeah. It's about why I think that students at this school eat lunch in their cars instead of on campus. You're going to ask what's my point. My point is that people don't feel like they're a part of the school, you know?
turn at talk #3 — · ➤	H^T: Yeah, I know what you mean.

TUTORING OPTIONS

45

An option, on the other hand, is a statement with one intent. Many times in tutoring, several options are used within one turn at talk. In the following example, the tutee asks a question ("How am I doin'?") and then replies ("Terrible! That's how I'm doin'.") to that question in the same turn: one turn at talk, two options used.

> one turn,
> two options   − · →   A: How am I doin'? Terrible! That's how I'm doin'.

OPTIONS USED BY BOTH TUTORS AND TUTEES

Please also keep in mind that tutees as well as tutors use all six options. Tutees ask questions, answer them, provide additional information, wait for others to talk, and so forth just like tutors do. However, because this book is intended for tutors like you, the focus is tutor behavior. Finally, please keep in mind that these options aren't a list of behaviors some researchers dreamed up, they are carefully derived descriptions of what tutors and tutees were observed to do in scores of tutoring sessions. This section on options is not a list of commandments, rather a practical guide to conceptualize your options as you make good tutoring decisions. Knowing these options will help you achieve the goals of tutoring as discussed in Chapter 1 and to reinforce learning processes as explained in Chapter 2.

TWO BENEFITS

Knowing the six options helps you in two major ways. First, these options provide a vocabulary for tutoring, allowing you to reflect on your experiences and plan to increase, decrease, or modify your behaviors in concrete terms. Perhaps if you are aware that you over explain — use too many additions — you can consciously set out to compensate. Second, during most tutoring sessions there are a few key moments where your decisions about what to say influence the direction of the rest of the session. At these key moments, it is critical to the success of the session to be more thoughtful about what you say.

SITUATIONS

As mentioned earlier, brief descriptions of actual tutoring situations are interspersed throughout this chapter. They are intended to help you apply what you are learning and to improve your ability to conceive of alternative ways of dealing with troublesome circumstances. As in previous chapters, the situations present the problem, but not the solution. There is no single right answer to these situations, but some answers are preferable to others. Some version of these situations has occurred to tutors at nearly every tutoring center in the country's colleges and schools. If not otherwise specified, please assume that the subject of the tutoring session is whatever subject you tutor. For example, if you tutor Algebra 1, then the situation occurs in an Algebra 1 tutorial. For your convenience, each situation is numbered and given a title.

Notes:

EXERCISE: 3-1 THE F-KEY

You have been tutoring Helena once a week for five weeks. She came to you after failing the first of two midterms. For the last few weeks you have been focused on helping her get ready for the second midterm. You are waiting for her to arrive for her weekly session. You know that since your last session, she has taken the second midterm and that the teacher has graded and returned it. You are about to find out how she did. Helena arrives, slams her books on the table and blurts out, "I flunked the test and it's your damned fault! You told me I was ready and that I'd do fine. You got me an 'F!' Are you satisfied now?!" You are stunned because you and Helena have had an excellent working relationship.

Write here exactly what you would say to Helena: _____

_____

What is your rationale for this statement? _____

_____

_____

OPTION 1: INITIATION

An initiation intends to cause a response. Initiations include what we typically think of as questions: an inverted subject and verb and rising inflection. An example might be, "Is this homework difficult?" Note the two classical characteristics of questions. First, the verb "is" and the noun "homework" are reversed from their usual noun verb order in a sentence. Second, that the question mark indicates a rise in inflection; the word "difficult" is said with the voice rising. Of course, a question can frame a statement. Initiations can also include any statement, command, or unfinished statement which intends to elicit some reply. Initiations *begin* a sequence and so have considerable influence on the direction of talk.

OPTIONS FOR TUTOR TALK

- ☑ INITIATE
- ☐ REPLY
- ☐ EVALUATE
- ☐ EXPLAIN
- ☐ ACTIVE LISTENING
- ☐ QUIET

Following are examples from transcripts of tutoring sessions. Underlining indicates initiations. The superscripted "T" (for example, J^T) identifies the tutor.

Old-fashioned question. In the first example, the tutor, "J," uses a typical initiation.

EXAMPLE 1

J^T: <u>How has the grammar class been going</u>?
C: I've been having trouble with conjugating those verbs.

Her statement is a question in which the subject "the grammar class" and the helping verb "has" are inverted and the sentence ends on a rising inflection as indicated by the question mark. Thus we call it an initiation.

Prompt. In the second example, the tutor, Gloria, initiates by giving an incomplete sentence and then pausing, signaling to the tutee, Mike, that he is expected to complete the sentence.

EXAMPLE 2

G^T: <u>OK, and the arrangements that have to be made by the person and the family are</u> (pause)
M: Uh (pause) are particularly difficult right after a loved one dies.

Between the tutor and the tutee, the complete sentence is "and the arrangements that have to be made by the person and the family are particularly difficult right after a loved one dies." By stating the first half and pausing, the tutor caused the tutee to state the second half. We know it's an initiation because the tutor and tutee treated it as one. Keep in mind that the intent of the statement to elicit a response is the deciding factor in labeling a statement an initiation, not its grammatical structure,.

Command. In the third example, the tutor issues what is essentially **a command**, "Tell me . . ." Again we know that this statement is an initiation because the tutor and tutee treat it as one. The tutee replies by completing the sentence the tutor started.

EXAMPLE 3

T^T: <u>Please tell me again what a thesis statement is</u>.
J: It's one statement which . . .

The tutor, Terry, expects that Julius will comply with her request to tell what a thesis is. The tutee in fact does comply, "It's one statement which . . ." Remember, some questions frame a statement; it's important to keep in mind that question inflection is not necessarily an indication of a question.

Problem statement. Another type of initiation is a **problem statement**, which indicates a trouble spot for the speaker. The problem statement does not directly tell the listener to do anything about it, yet the underlying intent of such a statement is to prompt a response. In the following dialog, Irma, the tutee, states that she doesn't understand something. We can see that the tutor, Sylvia, treats Irma's statement as an initiation because Sylvia responds to it.

EXAMPLE 4

I: <u>I don't understand. Like when I was looking at this I think I got more confused</u>.

S^T: Ok, if the price rises, if it's inelastic, the revenue's gonna (pause)

I: the revenue's gonna rise too. In other words . . .

MORE EFFECTIVE INITIATIONS

Linguistic flexibility. Incidentally, Sylvia's response is clever, a good example of linguistic flexibility being employed to empower the tutee. She starts to answer, then pauses, giving Irma the space to formulate the answer. This gives Irma the power of coming up with the answer rather than the passivity of just receiving it. So in the above dialog, Sylvia uses her understanding of tutorial options. Sylvia does not answer a question with a question of her own. This gives the tutee the help she needs to generate the answer. Further, by giving part of the answer ("if it's inelastic, the revenue's gonna…") Sylvia is giving some help, but still giving Irma the opportunity to help herself.

Notes:

Degree of influence. Like a serve in a tennis game, initiations exert influence on the person to whom they are directed. If a tutor asks a tutee to do or say something, then that tutor is influencing the tutee. More effective initiations use an economical influence — just enough to keep tutees on track and moving forward. The more influence you exert, the more you put the tutee in a subservient role. Subservience is contrary to your goal to empower the tutee, so more effective initiations reflect a "minimum intrusion - maximum gain" philosophy. Tutors exercise just enough influence and no more.

EXERCISE: 3-2

Review the sample dialogs for Option 1: Initiation (examples 1-4). List the number of the initiations below putting them in descending order of influence. List the most influential initiation first, the second most influential second, and so forth. Influence refers to the amount of choice an initiation allows the responder. "State your name" exerts more influence than "Shall we introduce ourselves."

1st Most Influential = # _____

2nd Most Influential = # _____

3rd Most Influential = # _____

4th Most Influential = # _____

EXERCISE: 3-3

Write down five initiations which you might use in your tutoring. Rank these initiations from most influential to least using #1 for the most, #2 for the next most, and so forth.

_____

_____

_____

_____

_____

EXERCISE: 3-4

Compare your list of initiations with another tutor's list. Working together, place both sets into the same list ranking most influential to least in descending order. You should have ten initiations on your list. The first is the most influential, the tenth is the least influential.

1. _____

2. _____

3. _____

4. _____

5. _____

6. _____

7. _____

8. _____

9. _____

10. _____

OPTION 2: REPLY

A reply is a response to an initiation. If somebody says something, which cannot be traced directly to a previous initiation, then it is not a reply. By definition, then, a reply cannot be identified independently of an initiation. While not all questions are followed by replies, all replies are preceded by initiations. The following is an example of a reply from a tutoring session in chemistry:

> L: Yeah. This is the glycerol. And what's this supposed to be? Is that part of the acid, the lipid, the fatty acid?
>
> C^T: Um, uh, oh boy. Essentially, yeah it would be. I think you could look at it that way. I think I'm being correct.

The tutee, Lorna, asks about a component of a molecule and the tutor, Carla, attempts to answer.

OPTIONS FOR TUTOR TALK

☑ INITIATE

☑ REPLY

❑ EVALUATE

❑ EXPLAIN

❑ ACTIVE LISTENING

❑ QUIET

Here's another example:

> K[T]: What steps did you take to solve that problem?
> L: Well, first I . . ."

The tutor, Kateesha, asks the tutee, Lois, to explain the steps to solve a problem. The tutee replies by beginning to list the steps.

Even if the reply is incorrect, incomplete, or inappropriate, it is still a reply, as in this example:

> P: So I'm not sure what I was supposed to do here.
> B[T]: <u>I'm not sure either</u>.

In this case, the tutor isn't able to answer the tutee's initiation, but still replies when he says, "I'm not sure either."

EXERCISE: 3-5 Now You See Me, Now You Don't

Fred finally shows up for a tutoring session with you. This is the fourth session he has scheduled with you in the last five weeks. He didn't show up at all for two of them and was almost fifteen minutes late for another. He has never called to cancel or indicate he would be late. In that one session for which he was late, he didn't seem very prepared. He didn't have his assignment with him, his class notes were erratic and written on all kinds of paper, and he indicated that he "sometimes missed class." He is affable and cooperative. Fred comes in 15 minutes late, sits down, and says, "Hi, how are you doing?"

How do you reply to Fred? _____

_____

What is your rationale for this statement? _____

_____

_____

MORE EFFECTIVE REPLIES

The two most important considerations in replying effectively are: (a) to focus on underlying strategies as discussed in Chapter 2, Steps 4 and 8; and (b) to avoid explaining too much. As you recall from Chapters 1 and 2, **focusing on learning strategies** helps tutees improve their abilities to direct their own learning, which is one of the fundamental goals of tutoring. Helping them learn strategies for learning promotes independence.

Thorough explanations help make the tutee more dependent. By definition, if you are doing the explaining then the tutee isn't. Your lengthy explanations deprive your tutees of the opportunity to work out answers for themselves.

Many effective tutors follow up a short reply with a pause — the option of quiet — or with an initiation. Whether you pause or wait, the expectation is that the tutee will do something: reply to your initiation, continue your explanation, or come up with another initiation. In any event, you're putting the ball in the tutee's court, rather than controlling the game yourself. Thus if you launch into a long reply to a tutee's question, you are preventing the tutee from working out parts of the answer. Further, you are training the tutee to be passive.

ANALYSIS OF "EXERCISE 3-5: NOW YOU SEE ME, NOW YOU DON'T"

The situation with Fred is a good opportunity to use the option of active listening effectively. At the end of the situation, Fred has asked the tutor, "How are you?" A short reply followed by waiting will give Fred the opportunity to speak about his unreliable attendance. A tutor might say, "I'm all right, thanks." Then the tutor waits. Wait until Fred talks. See if Fred says something about being tardy. If Fred says something about being late, then you can stay on that topic. He might say, "Sorry I'm late." Then you can say something like, "I'm glad you mentioned it because it is a problem for me." Then Fred can respond to your statement and you can stay on the topic until it is worked out.

Suppose Fred doesn't say anything about being late after you say, "I'm all right, thanks." Instead Fred says, "Well I need help with . . ." You will have to initiate by introducing the topic of Fred's unreliability. Be direct and honest. Focus on your concerns. You might say, "Before we start, I'd like to talk about missed and late appointments. The problem for me when you miss an appointment or are late is that I've saved this time for you. Other students

Notes:

avoid explaining too much . . . . . if you launch into a long reply . . . . . you are preventing the tutee from working out parts of the answer . . . . . you are training the tutee to be passive.

would like this time to meet with me, but they can't when you're already signed up." You might cite your own need to study and the limited time you have.

No matter what you say, use the option of quiet to give Fred the time to talk. Then when Fred does talk, listen actively by using the active listening option. Be open to what Fred has to say, but make sure he understands your situation as well. Stay with the topic until you and Fred agree to keep appointments and be on time. You have every right to communicate this expectation to Fred. If Fred's reliability continues to be a problem, speak with your supervisor. Your supervisor is paid to handle these types of problems.

OPTIONS FOR TUTOR TALK
☑ INITIATE
☑ REPLY
☑ EVALUATE
☐ EXPLAIN
☐ ACTIVE LISTENING
☐ QUIET

OPTION 3: EVALUATION

An evaluation option judges information, processes, relationships, or people. In tutoring, positive evaluations reinforce work well done or progress being made. Negative evaluations serve to continue the given topic, signaling that the tutor and tutee need to continue to work to produce a correct or satisfactory answer. As will be explained, evaluations are tricky and more effective tutors use them sparingly and carefully.

The following segment contains two evaluations: one by the tutor, Ricardo, and one by the tutee, Andre. Ricardo's evaluation indicates that the tutee accurately summarized the points of an essay in his concluding paragraph. Andre's evaluation reflects on the tutoring process as well as on his progress when he says, "Oh boy, we're gettin' somewhere."

R^T: Can you understand why I said that?
A: That summarizes everything I just got through talking about.
R^T: <u>That sounds about right</u>. Summarizes everything you just
    got through talking about.
A: ((mumbles)). ((laughs)) <u>Oh boy, we're gettin' somewhere</u>.
    <u>The end of the story.</u>

POWER OF EVALUATIONS

Evaluations are tricky for tutors. On the one hand, they serve as positive reinforcement. They help tutees know they are on the right track and help them feel good about their efforts. The tutor knows the information better than the tutee and so can better judge the accuracy and appropriateness of the tutee's efforts. Further, being on the right track and feeling good lead to an increased willingness to keep going ahead.

On the other hand, because the power to evaluate rests much more with the tutor than with the tutee, evaluating tutees gives you the potential to exert tremendous power over them. So, ironically, giving lots of positive evaluations to a tutee to help build confidence may make the tutee dependent on you. Therefore it's important that you employ the power to evaluate judiciously and thoughtfully.

This is true for both positive and negative evaluations. Superficial or excessive praising undermines your credibility and makes the tutee feel patronized. "Gee, John, you're doing so well in opening that book to the right page." Excessive criticizing will likely make your tutees defensive. "Why would you want to do that?"

POSITIVE EVALUATIONS

Positive evaluations are most effective when they are tied to specific aspects of a student's work and are used sparingly for real accomplishments. Let's look at this assertion one part at a time.

Specific aspects of a student's work means that an evaluation is directly related to something specific that the student did. Ever got a paper back from a teacher with the comment, "Good paper" on it? Your problem was figuring out what it was that you did that was good so that you can do it (whatever it is) next time. You know the teacher approved, but you can't learn much from the comment. If, instead, the teacher had indicated what specifically was "good" and why, then you know to do the same kind of thing in the future. Thus, a wise teacher might write, "This is a good example to include in this paragraph because . . ." The positive comment is specifically tied to the students' work.

The same is true for you: tie your positive evaluation to something specific that the tutee did. This accomplishes your basic goal of promoting independence in two ways. First, it clearly identifies your evaluation as being related to the student's work, as opposed to being related to the student's worth. You're not evaluating him; you're evaluating some identified aspect of his work. This helps depersonalize the evaluation. Once depersonalized, the amount of power wielded by an evaluator is significantly reduced.

Second, tying the evaluation to some specific aspect of the student's work helps him learn how to recognize specifically what he is doing right. Thus, the student becomes more independent, which is one of your fundamental goals in tutoring.

TUTORING OPTIONS   55

EXERCISE: 3-6

Write down some positive evaluations which are specifically tied to student's work. Compare what you write down with that of some of your fellow tutors. Expand your repertoire by learning from others. Remember that business about linguistic flexibility? Here's a chance to enhance your skills in this area.

Your evaluations _____

_____

_____

Praise used sparingly for real accomplishments means that you avoid the cloying and condescending quality of praising every little thing the student does. Hyper-praise does not help the student feel the satisfaction of genuine accomplishments and makes him/her more dependent on you for approval and acceptance. I know that this advice contradicts the often-heard adage, "Praise often and liberally." While this belief is common, it is misguided.

Praise doesn't motivate nearly as powerfully as success. Praise focuses on the person being praised more than the task and reinforces a dependency on others for one's own sense of well-being. Think about the things you enjoy doing. Whether your favored activities are gardening, writing poetry, working on cars, composing symphonies for sousaphones, playing basketball, reading, or cooking rutabagas, aren't they things you feel you do well?

Now, think about the things you don't like to do. Aren't they things that you feel you don't do well? All of us — tutors, teachers, tutees — tend to avoid things at which we don't succeed and to pursue things at which we do succeed. The point is that success at a task, not the approval of others, motivates us most powerfully. Feelings of success and ability, not the artificial prop of excessive praise, permanently under gird intellectual and personal development.

EXERCISE: 3-7 Thanks for helping . . . NOT!

This is the first time you've tutored Olga. She tells you that she has been receiving mostly D's on tests and assignments for her class. You begin to go over the material with her. Your impression is that she doesn't understand the material very well. The problem is she argues over every point you try to make. You are trying to be patient and oriented to the task at hand, but her arguing is making the session very difficult. Finally, progress has stalled completely while she argues with a fact in the textbook. You have to say something.

What do you say to Olga? _____

_____

What is your rationale for this statement? _____

_____

_____

NEGATIVE EVALUATIONS

If you think positive evaluations are tricky, try negative! How can you say that a tutee's effort is inaccurate or off the mark without discouraging the tutee? Aren't you sometimes obligated to tell a tutee whether he's right or not? The worst example of an evaluation I have ever encountered occurred when a tutor attempted to help a tutee with pronoun agreement exercises for an English grammar class. The dialog went as follows:

O: Okay, I think the answer is "Each member of the all male committee gave *their* report at the meeting."

S^T: No, no, no, no, no, no, no, no!

The exercises required the student to use the correct pronoun. The sentence the student was working on was, " Each member of the all male committee gave [his/their] report." In this case, the subject of the sentence was "each" which is singular, meaning the answer should be a singular pronoun, in this case "his." The tutee, "Oscar," gives an incorrect answer, "their," and the tutor, "Sherry," evaluates that answer.

Eight times Sherry said "no." How do you think Oscar felt? You won't be surprised to hear that as the session progressed, he became more tentative in his answers and more passive as he tried to avoid situations in which he would be at risk. And he was at risk any time he might have to produce an answer! In the extreme, therefore, we can see that negative evaluations can be defeating and counterproductive, making the tutee less, not more, able. So how do you let a tutee know he is on the wrong track?

Smaller steps. One technique used by more skillful tutors when a tutee produces an incorrect answer is to **break the current task into smaller steps** and ask a question about the first step. Thus, in the example of the grammar tutor, Sherry could have asked Oscar to identify the subject of the sentence. Once Oscar stated that "each" was the subject, then she could have asked him to indicate whether "each" was singular or plural. Then Sherry could ask Oscar whether his original answer, "their" was singular or plural.

Through this series of questions, the tutor could have avoided a negative evaluation and instead demonstrated an *approach* to doing all items in the exercise set: first identify the subject, then identify it as singular or plural, and then pick a pronoun which matches. In this way the tutor could help Oscar learn how to do this type of problem, enabling him to produce answers as a result of his own efforts.

Focus on progress. A second technique used by more skillful tutors is to identify **what was right** and to reinforce that. This is not to say that you create something phony to praise, but that you actually become more skillful in identifying the progress a student is making as he gets closer to a right answer or effective problem solving strategy. For example, if Fred were learning to swim, a teacher wouldn't criticize his stroke based on Olympic-level standards. Instead, the teacher would likely provide positive evaluation in regards to the progress Fred is making. A segment from a tutoring session in a composition class illustrates a negative evaluation that does *not* build on a positive:

L^T: Ellen, your example doesn't work for me. It seems a bit off the subject from the main idea of your paragraph.

Like the aspiring swimmer, Ellen knows she didn't do the example correctly. The tutor, Louis, could instead focus on what *is* right about the example. Why not reinforce Ellen's progress? Louis could indicate to her that the example is in exactly the right place in the paragraph and could then ask her how she knew to put an example there. Once Ellen has explained how she knows to include examples, *then* Louis can introduce the question of appropriateness of the example. Who knows? Maybe if Ellen has the *opportunity* to think — and then talk about her example, she will identify reservations she has about her example. Focusing on what is right enables tutees to see what they have done correctly and to feel a measure of success at their tasks.

Notes: ✍

EXERCISE: 3-8

Pause a moment and give some thought to the question: What could Louis have said to Ellen which would emphasize the positive?

_____

_____

What else could a tutor say to accomplish the same result?

_____

_____

_____

Let's return to our struggling grammar student, Oscar, to whom Sherry said "no" eight times. Instead, Sherry could say something like, "Tell me how you got that answer," then Oscar has the opportunity to explain and perhaps initiate discussion about what he doesn't understand. The focus of the tutoring session could shift away from Sherry hovering, waiting to attack a wrong answer, to a session in which Oscar can point out what exactly he doesn't understand and get help with that. You may be wondering, "But shouldn't I sometimes tell a tutee that an answer is not correct?"

When to give a negative evaluation. To answer, let's look at Oscar's incorrect answer, "Each member of the all male committee gave *their* report." Now, even though Oscar has just answered this item in the exercise set, Sherry asks Oscar another question about *that same item*. What does that tell Oscar? It tells him that he doesn't have it right yet, but instead of focusing on the fact that it is wrong ("no" eight times), it focuses on ways to get it right. When a tutor stays on the same task even when an answer has been posed, it's generally a signal that the answer is incomplete or inaccurate.

So, the question about when to give a negative evaluation isn't really the issue. The issue is behaving in ways that give tutees the opportunity to correct their own mistakes and to indicate areas where they need help. By re-conceptualizing your role in this way, you take yourself out of the evaluator role and put yourself into a facilitator role.

While evaluations are the least frequently employed option, they are powerful and important. Used sparingly and tied clearly to students' work, evaluations help students know what they are doing right and what needs more work. Misused, evaluations heighten tutors' power over tutees and undermine collaborative relationships by being either too judgmental or hyper-supportive.

OPTION 4: EXPLANATIONS

Explanations are statements that a tutor or tutee gives even though they weren't directly requested. Sometimes tutors and tutees just need to explain something. No one asked, but we know some information may be useful to fill in blanks, clarify, illustrate, summarize, or extend ideas. Explanations are often introduced by words that announce further explanation (and, but, so, in other words, what I mean to say is, what I hear you saying is).

Explanations are not initiations because their function is not to prod a reply. They are not replies because they are not responses to initiations. Explanations occur because of one's anticipation of what the other needs to know or because one is trying to clarify an idea. A significant amount of tutorial talk involves explaining ideas by elaborating, illustrating, or summarizing.

OPTIONS FOR TUTOR TALK

- ☑ INITIATE
- ☑ REPLY
- ☑ EVALUATE
- ☑ EXPLAIN
- ☐ ACTIVE LISTENING
- ☐ QUIET

EXAMPLES

The following examples illustrate the concept of explanation.

C: You have to explain this. I didn't understand what this was talking about (pause) (pages turning) (pause)

J^T: Do you have your handouts? (pause)

C: Umm yeah, that's for the lobster example <u>and he said we're gonna have lots of the same stuff on the test.</u>

J^T: Ah.

C: <u>OK and he said it won't be the same but the questions will be generally the same and we have to know how to answer them.</u>

Charlotte's first underlined statement is not an answer to a previously occurring initiation, and it doesn't initiate a tutor response. It provides more information than the tutor requested and at the same time supplies some context for Charlotte's earlier initiation — "You have to explain this." Her explanations provide a reason why the tutor has to "explain this." Further, the explanations are signaled in both instances by the conjunction "and." The "and" announces that more information is going to be offered.

In this next excerpt, Marcus' underlined explanation about pronoun agreement (people with they) was not a reply to an initiation. He was elaborating — volunteering additional information.

M: But I don't see how people or person was different.

G^T: Well that's a good one.

M: It should be people?

G^T: Right, because you're saying they.

M: Ah. <u>I can either say, when a person finds out he or she is going to die he or she goes through many changes before he or she can cope with it, or I can say when people find out they are going to die they go through many changes before they can cope with it.</u>

G^T: Right.

Immediately following Marcus' tentative guess about how to change that portion of his essay ("It should be people?"), Gloria confirmed it ("Right") and briefly explained why. Then Marcus elected to supplement with a lengthy explanation as to why the word "people" should be inserted into his paper. This supplemental information is an explanation.

<u>Summarizing.</u> The following is an excellent example of a very useful communication skill: summarizing. Summarizing re-states the essence of an idea so as to check understanding or highlight certain parts.

H: <u>So what I think I'm trying to say here is that there were lots of reasons why World War One started. But, you know there's one important reason people overlook, you know?</u>

W^T:Yeah

H: <u>And that is</u> . . .

In this example, the tutee, Harold, summarizes the point he is trying to make about one overlooked cause of World War One. In this tutoring session, more than five minutes of discussion had preceded this summary. Harold's strategy was to refocus what he was trying to say and make it clearer. He and the tutor had discussed the idea extensively but hadn't summarized the main point he was trying to make.

In this next example, the tutor summarizes what he thinks the tutee has been saying. In this case, the summary helps move the tutoring session forward. The tutor was afraid that if he didn't stop to summarize, the tutee would keep re-explaining his frustration but not move forward.

V^T: <u>So what I hear you saying is that you're really frustrated with this class and are really worried about your course grade.</u>

In this case, the tutor can move the session forward and signal his attention to the tutee's concerns.

FUNCTIONS OF EXPLANATIONS

Both tutors and tutees learn to anticipate information the other might need and so utilize explanations. Further, both tutors and tutees have occasion to summarize what has just been covered, to extend an idea, to provide examples of points they want to make, and to generate comparisons and analogies. The label "explanation" covers these components of talk. They reflect our fundamental desire to share our experiences and thoughts with other human beings. Within the context of tutoring, explanations provide an opportunity for tutors and tutees to learn from each other, to build ideas collaboratively, and to offer alternative explanations.

Explanations are a wonderful tool for tutors because they are not as imposing as initiations and are more conversational. Explanations have qualities of sharing and of cooperation. They help us see alternative avenues and points of view. Explanations serve at least eight functions in tutorials.

<u>1. Background</u>. Explanations can provide useful background information. Tutors and tutees often give each other pieces of background information. It is a way of giving more context to the discussion and to the relationship. When a tutee asks a question, for example, she may provide a reason for asking the question or explain why the question is important. When discussing the Harlem Renaissance of the early 20th Century, for example, a tutee might tell of a previous visit to Harlem or of a television documentary on the subject.

<u>2. Summarize</u>. Explanations can summarize what has been said. Such summaries help reinforce information ("So basically, the important thing is . . . ") or give a sense of the direction the session is going ("So where we are now is . . . ").

3. <u>Mirror</u>. Explanations can act as a mirror, in which a tutor can help a tutee understand messages the tutee is sending. For example, imagine Carlita, a tutee, talking about how hard her philosophy class is and about how much time she spends trying to decipher the reading assignments and so forth. A tutor who wishes to show Carlita the frustration she is communicating might say, "It can be really frustrating." Such a statement shows Carlita that her tutor is listening actively and is concerned about her state of mind. Further, Carlita can then see that she is communicating frustration and can decide what to do about it.

4. <u>Extend</u>. Explanations can build on what has been said, like a cooperative brainstorming session. Imagine the excitement of a situation where both you and your tutee are building on each other's ideas, refining and developing an increasingly sophisticated concept or approach to a problem. Each of you feels that you have contributed; each of you is valuing the contributions of the other. Together you are working cooperatively to produce insights beyond what you could have done individually. In addition, you are helping the tutee feel empowered because she is an equal partner in extending information.

5. <u>Missing piece</u>. Sometimes an explanation provides a valuable bit of new information that helps the tutee fit disparate parts together into a complete idea. You know that feeling of there being a missing piece? If you could just lay your hands on it, you could complete the puzzle in your mind. Sometimes an explanation can provide that piece. This reflects a "here's something that may help" approach to tutoring.

6. Comparisons. Sometimes metaphors, similes, analogies can help us better understand an idea. The metaphor of a puzzle in the preceding paragraph is an example. By comparing a type of thinking to putting together a picture puzzle, we can better understand that type of thinking. Comparisons therefore use what is understood to help us understand something new. Jane, a tutor for an economics class, compared the concept of elasticity to an elastic waistband. Elasticity refers to the degree to which consumers will still purchase specific goods and services in the face of price increases: the more elastic, the greater the variance in consumer purchasing of the product. Insulin is inelastic because it is essential for diabetics to balance the blood sugar levels in their systems. On the other hand, the demand for ice cream is elastic because people will buy more if the price drops and less if the price rises. With the elastic waistband analogy, Jane and Charlotte were able to discuss demand and consumption by comparing them to stomach size and waistband stretch.

7. Devil's advocate. Sometimes it's useful to present opposing points of view in tutoring. By playing devil's advocate, a tutor can help tutees sharpen and clarify their ideas.

8. Alternatives. Hearing other ideas, perspectives, approaches, or experiences can introduce tutees to other approaches to learning. "Another approach I've seen people use to write this kind of essay is . . ." Presenting alternatives can help tutees broaden their understanding of ideas and experiences. So for example, a non-African American tutee could be encouraged to take this perspective: "OK, I'm a college aged African American watching Martin Luther King's "I Have a Dream Speech" on television. What I think and feel is . . ." As this example intends to illustrate, explanations can facilitate understanding of powerful forces from new perspectives.

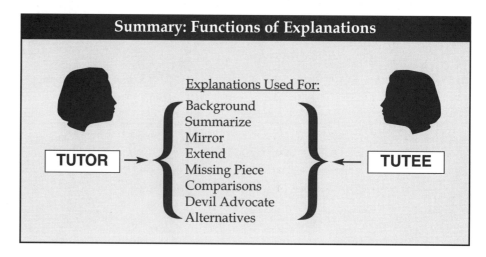

Summary: Functions of Explanations

TUTOR →

Explanations Used For:
Background
Summarize
Mirror
Extend
Missing Piece
Comparisons
Devil Advocate
Alternatives

← TUTEE

EXERCISE: 3-9 "Playing for the Assist and Not for the Score"

This is your second tutoring session with Lucas, a 32-year-old who came back to school for a new career after injuring his non-writing hand in a work accident. He asks good questions, listens very attentively, tries to write down as much of what you say as he can, and is very complimentary of your knowledge. You're pleased he is happy with your tutoring but suddenly, half way through this session and halfway through your answer to one of Lucas' questions, you realize you're doing nearly all the explaining.

What do you say to Lucas? _____

_____

What is your rationale for this statement? _____

_____

_____

EFFECTIVE EXPLANATIONS

Explanations are a wonderful tool for tutors because they are not as imposing as initiations. Explanations also have qualities of sharing and of cooperation. They help us see alternative avenues and points of view. Research and experience has shown us several conclusions about more effective explanations.

More effective tutors *show more flexibility* in using the various functions of explanations as discussed in the preceding paragraphs. More effective tutors *follow explanations with quiet or initiations* so as to encourage tutee talk. When you stop talking the tutee can talk. As a tutoring session progresses, more effective tutors *explain less and less*. Finally, more effective tutors *focus more often on underlying thought processes* than less effective tutors.

OPTION 5: ACTIVE LISTENING

A marker is a one-to-two-word turn at talk which signals active listening. Because the intent of a marker is to reinforce another's continued talking, they are timed so as to not interrupt the other's continued talk. The

OPTIONS FOR TUTOR TALK
☑ INITIATE
☑ REPLY
☑ EVALUATE
☑ EXPLAIN
☑ ACTIVE LISTENING
☐ QUIET

marker highlights the importance of very short statements like "OK," "Right," "Uh huh," and "Yeah." A tutor once succinctly summarized the role of marker statements as meaning, "I'm with you so far, go on." In other words, this active listening technique indicates acceptance of the direction the other's talk is taking.

PROVIDING OPPORTUNITIES

Because markers reinforce another's continued task, tutors can use them to provide opportunities for tutees to explain, discover, question, and discuss. If the tutee is actively engaged in talking about the content, then she is actively engaged in learning. While simple and very brief, active listening is a powerful tool in your tutoring toolbox. The use of markers signals that you are actively listening and keeps your tutee talking.

Here are a few examples. In this first example from a tutorial for an economics class, Charlotte, the tutee, uses markers to keep her *tutor* talking. Note how successful she is! Jane, the tutor, explains the concept of elasticity instead of helping Charlotte do the explaining. This is a good example of how powerful something as simple as an "Uh huh" is.

J^T: You stretch it
C: Uh huh
J^T: means it's more elastic
C: It stretches
J^T: Uh huh, so like in this example when the price rises
C: Uh huh.

Charlotte's "uh huh" served to keep Jane continuing her explanation of elasticity, despite Jane's training to promote the tutee's explanation.

EFFECTIVE ACTIVE LISTENING

The active listening technique of using effective markers: (a) **fits into the flow** of the other's talk without talking over the other, (b) occurs often enough to **show interest** and not so often as to be a distraction, and (c) **demonstrates sincerity**. Fitting into the flow involves a sense of rhythm and timing. The tutor inserts markers into the very short, mini-pauses that occur in our talk. Active listening requires appropriate markers. Here are two sample dialogs from a fictional tutoring session between Xavier and Frieda. In which dialog are markers more smoothly fit into the flow of talk?

Dialog 1

X^T: So you wanna tell me more about the term paper assignment?

F: Well, the first thing the teacher said is that in

X^T: Yeah

F: Uh, in the beginning, the most important thing is picking a

X^T: Uh huh

F: Uh, a topic.

Dialog 2

X^T: So you wanna tell me more about the term paper assignment?

F: Well, the first thing the teacher said

X^T: Yeah

F: Is that in the beginning, the most important thing

X^T: Uh huh

F: Is picking a topic.

In Dialog 1, Xavier inserts the marker, "Yeah" right in the middle of the phrase "in the beginning." In Xavier's next turn at talk, he makes the same type of mistake when he inserts "Uh huh" in the middle of the phrase, "picking a topic." Fortunately for Xavier he has a hand-held time machine and so after reading this chapter, he transports himself back to his tutoring session with Frieda.

This time in Dialog 2, he inserts "Yeah" between "the teacher said" and "is that." In this way he doesn't so much split what Frieda is trying to say as he fits it into one of those mini-pauses. Then, Xavier is poised again to insert a marker at a more appropriate place in the flow of talk. Frieda says, "the most important thing;" Xavier says, "Uh huh;" and then Frieda says, "Is picking a topic." Again, Xavier's marker fits into a mini-pause.

Trust your instincts. Active listening can be intuitive. Practice markers as part of your early training so that you can develop your active listening skill before you need it. Trust your instincts. You are probably doing a good job with markers already.

Notes:

Trust your instincts . . . . . You are probably doing a good job with markers already.

Here's a real example from an introductory psychology class of a tutor using markers to keep the tutee talking. Note that all the tutor does is say "OK;" the tutee does the rest. The tutor is actively listening, and simultaneously bridging the flow. This is a good example of empowering the tutee. Note that the tutee is allowed to talk without restriction, that the tutor provides just enough input to keep the tutee explaining, and that the tutee talks much more than the tutor.

> E: So the thing with Maslow
> N^T: <u>OK</u>
> E: Is the hierarchy of needs and stuff.
> N^T: <u>OK</u>
> E: Basically, he says that we have these needs and some come before,
>   er ah, (pause) are more important or basic I guess
> N^T: <u>OK</u>
> E: than others. So let's see (pause) like the need to stay alive and that
>   kind of thing is more important than the need to. . .

This tutor, Naomi, shows a great deal of skill in promoting Eric's active involvement in his own learning. First, she utilizes three markers (an "OK" each time) to show Eric that she is following his explanation thus far and he should keep going. Second, she showcases her skills on a much more subtle level by not speaking when Eric pauses.

In Eric's third and fifth turns at talk, he pauses in the middle of his explanation. Many tutors would have filled in those pauses with their own talk. In this case, had Naomi begun talking when Eric paused, she would be taking over the explanation and Eric would shift from being actively involved in his own learning to becoming the passive receptor of Naomi's explanation. Eric's first pause occurs when he stumbles a bit over how to say that according to Maslow's theory, some basic needs take precedence over others. He says, "some come before, er ah, (pause)." The "er ah" indicates some hesitation which is confirmed by the pause. At this point most tutors would be tempted to start talking in order to "help" Eric. Naomi is certainly eager to *help* Eric, but if her help took the form of filling in for him by continuing his explanation, then she will have actually *hindered* his active involvement in his own learning.

The second and third features of more effective markers are closely related. The second feature of effective markers is that they occur often enough to show active interest and not so often as to be annoying. The third feature of effective markers is that they are sincere. If you are sincerely interested in what your tutees say to you, then that interest will naturally manifest itself.

Generally, tutees' assessments of tutor insincerity occur because tutors try too hard, and if they try too hard, they are likely to overdo lots of things. For example, they will probably be too quick to offer explanations, too extravagant in their praise for tutees' efforts, and too lavish in their use of markers. The point is that by understanding what active listening does and how to use it effectively, tutors can help the tutee do more of the talking and thus more of the learning.

Option 6: Quiet

The sixth option available to you is quiet. **While it may seem that being quiet is doing nothing, when you are quiet you are actually giving the tutee the opportunity to do something.** Quiet is hard for tutors to do. You tend to feel responsible for helping the tutee and so want to do something. Whether what you do is explain, ask questions, or finish sentences the tutee starts, the fact is that, once you talk, the tutee is likely to stop talking. Once the tutee stops talking and you start, you become active and the tutee becomes passive.

Who Explains to Whom?

And what will you talk about? Observations of hundreds of tutoring sessions reveal that, when tutors talk, the overwhelming tendency is to explain course material to their tutees. And if tutors explain the material to tutees, then tutees are *not* explaining the material. Nor are they learning how to learn that material for themselves. Thus tutors who aren't good at being quiet are likely to be training their tutees to be dependent. Let's look at a couple of segments of tutoring sessions and see how this plays out.

> P: So basically the arteries carry blood away from the heart and veins carry it to the heart. So what's that got to do with blood pressure and wall thickness? (pause) Hmm.
> Y^T: Well, the thing with blood pressure has to do with the thickness of cell walls. (pause) Arteries have thicker walls because they're under more pressure.

Notes:

OPTIONS FOR TUTOR TALK
☑ INITIATE
☑ REPLY
☑ EVALUATE
☑ EXPLAIN
☑ ACTIVE LISTENING
☑ QUIET

P: The blood in veins kind of drifts back to the heart?
Y^T: Well they certainly aren't receiving the main, you know, push from the heart. The heart's like a pump . . .

In the first line of dialog from a biology tutorial, the tutee, Paul, pauses and then says "Hmm," after which the tutor, Yolanda, answers the tutee's question. In the middle of her explanation, Yolanda pauses. When Paul doesn't say anything, Yolanda does. Yolanda's talk consists of explaining the ideas to Paul. She is not providing Paul with the opportunity to work it out himself or to further explain his initial question ("So what's that got to do with blood pressure and wall thickness?"). She is inadvertently training Paul that the way for him to get answers is to not know. The less he knows the more she will tell him. Paul will probably rely less and less on himself and rely more and more on his tutor.

There's no guarantee that if Yolanda hadn't talked after Paul's original pause that Paul would have continued to talk. The point is that Yolanda will never know because she didn't give Paul the opportunity to talk. So there is some chance that Paul would talk after the pause, if he is given the time to do so. Quiet is instrumental in the learning process. If it is not given to him, there is no chance for Paul to work out his own question. Obviously, some chance is better than none. By being quiet, you give your tutees that chance and you will be subtly encouraging them to rely on themselves.

A tutee explains. Here's a second dialog from a sociology tutorial which shows a tutor, Trina, making effective use of the option of quiet to give Everett the time to clarify and elaborate.

T^T: What would you like to work on today?
E: I'm trying to work out what it is that W. E. B. DuBois said about social forces and groups (pause) and that kind of stuff. (pause) I mean I know that his theories . . .

Everett pauses twice and each time Trina was quiet and each time Everett continued to explain. Between the first pause and the second, Everett doesn't offer much solid information, "and that kind of stuff." It doesn't matter. After his second pause, he begins to tell what he does know! Telling what he does know about DuBois' theories is much more empowering than hearing what the tutor knows.

EXERCISE: 3-10

At the end of your next tutoring session, say something like this to your tutee. "I have an assignment for my tutor training class and I wonder if you could help me. Would you write down your honest assessment of how much I talked today in relation to how much you talked? I'm going to do the same, but let's not show each other what we write until after." Express your estimates as percents of time, like tutor talked 65% of the time, tutee talked 35% of the time.

Your tutee's estimate: Your estimate:
tutor talk: _____% tutee talk: _____%   tutor talk: _____% tutee talk: _____%

List below some steps you can take to increase the amount of tutee talk and reduce your talk. In your list utilize terms and concepts introduced in the Options Section of this chapter.

_____

_____

_____

_____

Providing opportunity. In addition to not filling in your tutees' pauses, the quiet option is also useful for giving tutees the option to talk after you, whether it is to expand on your idea, reply to your initiation, or offer their own ideas. In the following segment from a tutorial for a Spanish 2 class, the tutor, Estella, poses an initiation and gives her tutee, Carl, enough time to realize his mistake and to rely on his Spanish/English dictionary, not his tutor, for the answer.

E^T: Did you just use the word "embarazada" to mean "embarrassed?" (pause)

C: Oh that's right! (laughs) Embarazada means pregnant. Man! That changes the meaning! (pause) Let's see. (pause) Embarrassed. (He looks it up in the dictionary) Azorado!

E^T: Si, Azorado!

TUTORING OPTIONS   71

Estella first utilizes a pause after her initiation, "Did you just use the word 'embarazada' to mean 'embarrassed?'" This gave Carl the time he needed to figure out what the problem was *and* to fix it. He remembers that "embarazada" means pregnant. Then he pauses and Estella does nothing. Carl then realizes that he needs to know what the Spanish word is for "embarrassed" and he pauses again, but Estella still doesn't jump in to help Carl. He then looks it up in the dictionary. Estella's resistance to doing the work for Carl gives him the opportunity to achieve success based on his own efforts. Her quiet gave Carl the opportunity to learn.

EXERCISE: 3-11

In your next tutoring session, preferably with the same tutee as before, again get estimates of relative talk time in the same way as before. Write the results below:

<u>Your tutee's estimate</u>

tutor talk: _____%   tutee talk: _____%

<u>Your estimate:</u>

tutor talk: _____%   tutee talk: _____%

How successful were you in implementing your strategies and how much did these strategies alter the results?

_____

_____

_____

_____

_____

CONCLUSION

In this chapter you learned about six options for tutorial listening and talk. **Initiations** intend to cause a response. Many, but not all, initiations are in a question form. **Replies** are responses to initiations. **Evaluations** judge relationships, processes, information, or people. **Explanations** provide information that hasn't been directly requested. Explanations serve at least eight different functions. **Active listening** can be accomplished by using very short statements that reassure the tutee that you are paying attention. The **quiet** option involves respectfully and deliberately doing nothing so the tutee will do something.

Overall, the purpose of knowing these options is to be able to exert no more influence than is necessary to get tutees on track and keep them there. Less is more in effective tutoring. The overall goal is to provide opportunities for the tutee to succeed.

These options are nothing more than practical applications. If you reflect on your tutoring experiences and consider how to improve your craft, you will begin to see that these options provide you a very useful vocabulary for understanding the building blocks of your tutorial strategy. The process of discovering more about yourself as a communicator and the challenge of improving your capabilities is both deeply rewarding and intellectually stimulating. These options give you the power to unravel the complex dynamics of helping another learn and the ability to be more focused and successful in your tutoring.

Further, these options give you the power to modify your behavior to meet the main goals of tutoring. Whatever you do in tutoring affects the relationship you have with your tutees and influences how and what they learn. You must be cognizant of your actions and their consequences. Many of your tutees have not been well served by schools and the society in which they live. You are in a position to serve them well. Doing so provides students with access to all the benefits of higher education: personal growth, greater understanding of our world, respect for and joy in the worlds of differences and similarities among us, and increased opportunities for vocational and social advancements. You help students by being thoughtful and committed to what you do as a tutor.

Above all, remember that there is a strength to allowing a tutee's understanding to unfold. It is a great temptation to *tell* someone what something means. Learning is much more powerful and satisfying if it is a cognitive process. Your greatest tool may be the quiet pause that allows the tutee to think, and to learn.

Notes:

It is a great temptation to tell someone what something means . . . . . Your greatest tool may be the quiet pause that allows the tutee to think, and to learn.

74

CHAPTER 4:
TUTORING PATTERNS

 TUTORING
ROLE

 TUTORING
CYCLE

 TUTORING
OPTIONS

 **TUTORING
PATTERNS:**

 TUTORING
INTER-
CULTURALLY

CHAPTER 4: TUTORING PATTERNS

INTRODUCTION

In the first three chapters a great deal of information has been shared with you to help you make good decisions in your tutoring. In Chapter 1, you learned that adhering to the six goals of tutoring helps keep you and the tutees on track and keeps the tutees responsible for their learning. In Chapter 2 you learned about the Tutoring Cycle, especially Steps #4 and #8 which emphasize learning *how* to learn. In Chapter 3, you learned about the six options for tutoring talk: initiate, reply, evaluate, explain, active listening, and quiet. Chapter 4 is closely tied to Chapter 3. In Chapter 4, we will be concerned with the types of decisions made by more effective tutors in the course of a tutoring session.

RESEARCH BASED

The information in Chapter 4 is based on an extensive analysis of recorded tutoring sessions and of interviews with tutors and tutees. Prior to this research, many tutor trainers thought that asking questions was the essence of tutoring and that asking *good* questions was the essence of *good* tutoring. After all, in ancient Greece, Socrates utilized skillful questioning to lead a young boy to understand the principles of geometry. Similarly, the reasoning goes, modern-day tutors would also skillfully question students, leading them to profound insights into such things as the nature of allegorical meaning in literature, the mysteries of molecular structure in chemistry, the hierarchy of human needs in psychology, and the soul-stirring synthesis of harmony, melody, and rhythm in music composition. Much of tutor training, therefore, consisted of teaching questioning strategies to tutors.

When modern-day tutoring is carefully observed, however, the notion that tutors ask questions and tutees answer them was quickly dispelled. While it is true that tutors question and tutees reply, it is also true that *tutees* initiate and *tutors* reply. I don't want to sound like the vege-matic commercial, but wait, there's more! Not only do tutors and tutees question each other and reply to each other, they also explain to each other without having been directly asked to do so. Sometimes the tutees are doing most of the explaining and sometimes the tutors explain more. But wait! There's more! Sometimes neither is leading. Instead, each is building on information provided by the other. Tutoring is much more than asking good questions. In this chapter, we explore the main strategies that tutors and tutees have been seen to use. These strategies are derived from the tutoring behavoirs described in Chapter 3.

How Chapter 4 Is Organized

Notes: ✍

The information in this chapter is based on up-to-date and innovative research on the tutoring process. We are concerned with two questions:

1. What patterns in tutors' decision making have been observed?
2. What are the advantages and disadvantages of each pattern?

Chapter 4 is organized into two sections. The first is concerned with the Initiation and Reply Pattern; the second is concerned with the Explain and Active Listening Pattern. In each section are definitions, examples, and discussions of advantages and disdvantages. As in the other chapters of The Master Tutor: A Guidebook for More Effective Tutoring, exercises, situations, and sample dialogs supplement the content.

EXERCISE: 4-1

Pair up with another tutor. One of you will act as a tutor, the other as a tutee in a role play situation. The tutor picks the subject matter of the session and begins the session. The tutee's assignment in this role play is to continually attempt to get the tutor to do the explaining. The tutor, of course, must try to provide opportunities for the tutee to do the explaining. Limit your role play to 5 minutes. After the role play, talk about strategies the tutee used to get the tutor to do the explaining. Also, identify ways the tutor attempted to counter the tutee's efforts. List tutee strategies on the left and tutor counter-strategies on the right.

Tutee strategies	Tutor counter-strategies
_____	_____
_____	_____
_____	_____
_____	_____

Reverse roles. Repeat the role play. This time the tutor should attempt to utilize counter-strategies from your list. How well did the counter-strategies work?

OVERVIEW OF PATTERNS

Extensive research based on detailed analysis of many tutoring sessions has shown that there are two main patterns in tutoring interaction. As we learned in Chapter 3: Tutoring Options, tutors make moment-to-moment decisions about what to say and what not to say throughout any tutoring session. As we look at how these decisions add up over the course of sessions, we see that the choices tutors make influence the choices tutees make. In turn, the tutees' choices influence the choices tutors make. So as a session progresses each is influencing the other as each exercises one of the tutoring options.

The first pattern is called **IRP** for Initiation-Reply Pattern. After studying and analyzing which options people employ and how they occur in relation to each other, we see that initiations and replies seem to happen together. Over 70% of the time in tutoring, an initiation leads to a reply or to another initiation. This is no big surprise. By definition, an initiation seeks a reply. Thus, combinations of initiation and reply options constitute the first pattern.

The second pattern is called **EALP** for Explain-Active Listening Pattern. Approximately 70% of explanations are paired with other explanations or with active listening. So when there is an incidence of explanations or active listening, there is a great likelihood of more explanations and active listening and a low likelihood of questions and replies.

Incidentally, evaluations aren't a part of either pattern, because there are so few evaluations to start with. Evaluations by either the tutor or the tutee occur less than 7% of the time. As a result we won't be discussing evaluations in this chapter. To review information about evaluations, please see the appropriate section in Chapter 3.

Effective use of patterns. Briefly, the presence of these two patterns and the fact that they are so distinct from each other indicates that there are two basic ways of accomplishing tutoring. The first way is by initiating and replying. A second way of accomplishing tutoring involves active listening and explaining. *There are two keys to effective use of tutoring patterns.* The first is knowing **when** and **why** to use each pattern. The second is knowing **how** and **when** to cause the tutee to take the lead and stay on track in each pattern.

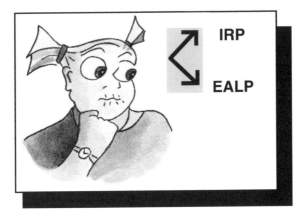

Notes: ✍

CHARACTERISTICS AND ADVANTAGES OF IRP

As stated earlier, the **Initiation-Reply Pattern (IRP)** consists of combinations of initiation and reply moves. Either the tutor or the tutee may be initiating and thus either can be replying.

<u>Example</u>. The following dialog illustrates a recurring cycle of tutor initiations and tutee replies. The tutor and tutee were trying to identify a chemical compound from its structural diagram.

tutee initiation	⟶	L:	OK. (pause) What is a lipid?
tutor initiation	⟶	C:	What is it?
tutee reply, initiation	⟶	L:	I dunno. I didn't understand it.
tutor initiation	⟶	C:	What's it say?
tutee reply	⟶	L:	It says it's a bimolecule which is not water soluble but it's soluble in organic solvents.
tutor initiation	⟶	C:	So a lipid, if you put a lipid in water it wouldn't dissolve, right?
tutee reply	⟶	L:	It's fat.

The tutor persisted in her strategy of leading questions and clues to prompt the tutee to answer, despite the tutee's initial effort to question the tutor and subsequent reply, "I dunno." Note that in the same turn as the "I dunno" reply, the tutee again initiated with a statement of need, "I didn't understand it." Although this initiation requested an explanation from the tutor, the tutor ignored it. Instead of replying the tutor also initiated, "What's it say?" This initiation leads the tutee to begin to answer the initiation.

Tutor initiates, tutee replies. Tutor's initiations are generally intended to provide an opportunity for the tutee to explain. Compared to active listening or a quiet option an initiation has a much stronger expectation that the tutee will do something with that opportunity. Skillful tutors usually use as little influence as possible until they have evidence indicating that more influence may be necessary. If the more subtle options of quiet or active listening don't work, then an initiation may be useful. Initiations exert more influence on the tutee than waiting for the tutee to talk or saying, "Uh huh." Therefore, initiations are usually used when the more subtle approaches of active listening and quiet haven't worked.

When the tutee does explain, there are still several advantages for you. First, you can attend carefully to the explanation to **assess** the tutee's knowledge. "Maybe you could review the steps in cell mitosis." As the tutee's explanation unfolds, you can learn what the tutee knows and about how the tutee approaches the task.

Second, initiating helps you **focus** the session on what needs to be done. "Your first question to me concerned economic causes of the Civil War. Shall we go over that first?" An initiation such as this helps get your session down to business while attributing credit for the topic to the tutee.

Third, your questions can also **model** a thinking process. Each initiation represents a step in the underlying thought process associated with completing a task. In a grammar class, for example, a tutor might ask the following sequence of questions. "What is the subject of the sentence?" "What is the verb?" "What are the prepositional phrases?" By repeating these questions each time a similar task is addressed, the tutee will learn to ask these questions and will also try to answer them. When the tutee is focusing his learning by asking and answering questions, then he is functioning independently.

Fourth, your initiations can **direct attention** to a new task or back to the task at hand. Imagine a physiology tutorial in which a tutee digresses by telling you about a wild party last weekend. You want to get the session back on track. You might say, "Sounds like a great party. Shall we work on the structure of nerve cells now?" This statement acknowledges the digression, but brings the session back to the physiology class.

Tutee initiates, tutor replies. In many instances, a tutee initiation says, in effect, "This is what I need to know." When this happens, the tutee is

TUTORING PATTERNS

actively involved in defining what is to be learned. A tutee's initiation has two advantages for you. First, it helps **direct you** to what the tutee needs to know. In this case, a tutee's initiation is an "I need help with . . ." statement. In a chemistry tutorial for example, a tutee might initiate as follows: "This section on calculating moles really confused me." This statement is an initiation because the tutee expects the tutor to answer and because tutors have a responsibility to help students find answers. So although it might not seem like it requires a reply, this statement has the force of an initiation.

Second, a tutee initiation **seeks clarification or direction** from you. "Is it true that 'connotation' refers to the feelings and ideas associated with a word and 'denotation' is the literal meaning?" In this instance, the tutee is differentiating between denotative and connotative word meanings and wants to be sure she is correct.

DISADVANTAGES OF IRP

If IRP has so many advantages, why don't tutors and tutees use it all the time? The answer is that there are at least five disadvantages. The existence of disadvantages, however, does not mean that you should avoid IRP. Instead, it means that you should be aware of them while you tutor and use your understanding of the advantages and disadvantages to help you make good decisions.

Good initiating is difficult. First, posing good questions *or* answering them well is **difficult**. Socrates subtly guided his students to exciting realizations through skillful questioning, but amateur tutors are not as likely to have developed such a skill. For tutors, instead of spiralling upwards to higher revelations, questioning is likely to deteriorate to a "guess what's in my head" game. To the tutee it can seem as though the tutor makes the following demand, "I'm thinking of something, guess what it is?"

Continued unsuccessful questioning can also take on the qualities of an interrogation, "Well, if you don't know A, do you know B?" "Well how about C?" "Where were you on the night of the murder?" It may seem to the tutee that he is trapped in a dank, sweaty cement-block room blinking at cigarette smoke drifting through a bright light aimed directly into his eyes, while a hard-boiled detective leans over him firing questions designed specifically to ensnare him.

Notes: ✍

Continued unsuccessful initiating is awkward. Second, when both the tutor and tutee know the questioner is asking questions to which the questioner already knows the answer, it becomes **awkward**. Only in instructional settings or in courtrooms can we find a situation where Person A asks B for information A already has. Most of us would not ask a question to which we already have the answer in other situations. Imagine, for example, that you drive into a gas station and ask the attendant for directions to the airport. Then, when he has completely explained, you say, "That's exactly right! Good for you!" You might want to have the car in gear ready to drive away quickly.

Cultural differences. **Third, questions are not used the same way in every group**. This is especially true for **some** Asian, African American, and Native American tutors or students. In white and middle-class groups, questions are used to elicit responses and are generally seen as an acceptable instructional strategy. Further, it is expected that a reply will be immediately given to an initiation.

In these next three paragraphs, please note that we are talking about the *possibility* that *some* individuals *may* act in the ways described. For this reason, you will see words such as "may," "might," and "some." These words have been carefully chosen. As you will learn in Chapter 5, individual members of any given cultural group cannot be assumed to have any of the experiences, attitudes, knowledge, or communication practices which might be ascribed to their group.

For some Native American cultures, for example, questions do not carry the expectation of a reply. The questioner assumes the other person will usually consider the question and then utilize it in whatever way he deems appropriate. A Native American tutor, therefore, may use questions in a different way than a middle-class white tutor. A Native American tutee may perceive questions differently than a white middle-class tutee.

For some Asian Americans, questions are not a part of an instructional strategy. Instead, learning may be achieved through careful recreation of what the teacher has explained. For some Asian American students, memorization and repetition can be the principal means for learning.

For some African American students, initiations may be seen as a threat. These individuals may have learned to mistrust the intent of initiations originating from outside their own immediate group. Thus, rather than seeing initiations as guides to discovering knowledge, these individuals perceive them as threatening to expose ignorance.

Feelings of resentment or inadequacy. Fourth, unsuccessful initiating can promote **feelings of inadequacy or resentment**. If a tutee is repeatedly unable to answer the questions you pose, then he may feel increasingly unable to achieve and increasingly dependent on you for help. "After all," the tutee's reasoning goes, "you know the answer to all these questions and I don't." Continued reliance on IRP as a way of accomplishing learning may make the tutee feel less able.

Sometimes inappropriate. Fifth, some information may be **exchanged best by simply stating it**. If one doesn't know that H stands for hydrogen, for example, then it is unlikely that posing questions will lead to that discovery. More importantly, the answer may not be worth an elaborate strategy for a succession of initiations.

CHARACTERISTICS AND ADVANTAGES OF EALP

Combinations of explanation and/or acitve listening options constitute a second pattern of interaction in instruction — **the Explain/Active Listening Pattern (EALP)**. The EALP offers you and the tutees a way to continue progressing toward an answer to the existing problem when initiating and replying have not worked. Sometimes the tutor explains (uses explanations) while the tutee actively listens. Other times the reverse is true: the tutee explains and the tutor listens. Sometimes, the tutor and tutee are both explaining, each building on or elaborating on the other.

Tutor explains, tutee actively listens. The tutor's explanation serves at least two purposes. First, a tutor's explanation sometimes signals the beginning of EALP. When you start to explain the tutee will likely attend closely. After all, you have information the tutee wants!

Second, in the beginning of an EALP, you can avoid the pitfalls of continued unproductive questioning. Sometimes, according to one tutor, "All the questions in the world aren't going to get the tutee to see the answer. When that happens, my job may be to explain a bit." The tutee, in turn, learned by attentive listening rather than by responding to questions (i.e. initiations).

Tutee explains, tutor actively listens. The tutee's explanations helps your tutoring in five ways. First, by adding information to that of the tutor, the tutee is **signaling you to stop** explaining. Given your goal of providing opportunity, a tutee's explanation represents the seizing of that opportunity. Second, the tutee is showing you a **good faith effort** to work out an answer. When she explains to you, she is showing you her effort to be independent. Third, your tutee may use EALP to **summarize** her learning or to summarize

> *"Sometimes, all the questions in the world aren't going to get the tutee to see the answer. When that happens, my job may be to explain a bit."*

the underlying learning process. These summaries represent tutoring success. At this point you are focused on the tutee's learning and the tutee is doing the explaining! Fourth, when tutees explain, **you can assess** the accuracy and completeness of the tutees' knowledge. Fifth, when the tutee explains, you have the opportunity to see what is being learned and how it is being learned from the **tutee's perspective**. This helps you understand and respect differences between you and your tutees.

Tutor and tutee explain. Sometimes both you and the tutee will be explaining, each building on the explanation of the other. When this happens you and the tutee may be functioning as approximately equal partners, each doing some of the explaining, each person's contribution building on that of the other.

The following is an example. The tutor is indicated by "J^T," the tutee is "C." The explanations help each understand the other; the tutor actively listening encourages the tutee's continued talk. Note, for example, that in the tutee's first turn, she adds the word "inelastic." After this the tutor provides an active listening option which encourages C's continued explanation. The pair of evaluations at the end of the segment indicate that each was satisfied with the outcome.

tutor explanation	⟶	J^T:	It's gonna be inelastic.
tutee explanation	⟶	C:	If it's very steep it's inelastic.
tutor actively listening	⟶	J^T:	Uh huh
tutee explanation	⟶	C:	Not very much change. The quantity doesn't change very much.
tutor explanation	⟶	J^T:	OK. That's getting back to what you were saying here.
tutee explanation	⟶	C:	There's a big difference.
tutor explanation	⟶	J^T:	And then that's responsive to prices.
tutee evaluation	⟶	C:	Right.
tutor evaluation	⟶	J^T:	Right. OK.

Interaction in an informational stage was characterized by explanation-active listing and explanation-explanation exchanges, as information is passed, acknowledged, summarized, or extended. Discussion of "inelastic" in the interaction above demonstrates how explanation and active listening behaviors fit together and promote learning.

<u>EALP and changes in the tutorial relationship</u>. You can utilize EALP to promote active learning. As tutees take over an explanation and as you utilize active listening to encourage it, the tutees will feel a sense of accomplishment as they explain what they have learned. *EALP is, therefore, an opportunity for participants to practice a role change from tutee dependence to independence.*

EXERCISE: 4-2

Imagine that you are tutoring Randall in an introductory political science class. You have been working with him to help him understand the differences between the concepts of "republic" and "democracy." You are about two-thirds through this session when you fear that you have made a mistake. You interrupted Randall's explanation with your own explanation. Dialog from this critical point is shown below.

tutor explanation →	You:	So that's what your notes and the book indicate about what a republic is. And what a democracy is. It's got to do with who participates in the actual governing.
tutee explanation →	Randall:	I get it! A republic is where representatives <u>represent</u> the people and the representatives do the governing for them! And in a true democracy
tutor explanation →	You:	Yeah! A true democracy is where all citizens participate in the governing directly, like a town meeting on a giant scale. So everybody is running it, but in a republic a few people are elected to run it for everybody.

What would you say next? Then, figure out what you would do to fix the situation, given that it has already happened.

_____

_____

_____

_____

_____

Notes: ✍

EALP is . . . . .
an opportunity
for participants
to practice a
role change
from tutee
dependence to
independence.

DISADVANTAGES OF EALP

The Explain-Active Listening Pattern is a powerful and useful approach for tutoring. It avoids many of the problems associated with the Initiation-Reply Pattern and provides opportunities for tutees to take the lead or to collaborate with tutors. There are, however, three disadvantages. Balancing the advantages against these disadvantages will help you utilize this pattern most effectively.

Off track. Sometimes exchanging information will take the tutee off track, and he or she will begin to talk about something other than the task at hand. When you give the tutee opportunities to explain, there's no guarantee that she will make perfect use of them. At some time or another, we all get off of the topic.

When a tutee does drift off topic, you will need to decide whether to intervene and, if so, how. Essentially, you would likely intervene when it becomes apparent to you that the tutee is not going to quickly move herself back on track. In other words, you give the tutee the opportunity to re-orient to the academic task, but if she doesn't, then you can help. To re-orient the tutee to the task, utilize IRP. See particularly the fourth advantage of the section entitled: "Tutor initiates, tutee replies." In the example in that paragraph, the tutor responds to the tutee's digression concerning a wild party.

Takeover. You can also be aware of when the tutee is ready to take over the explanation. It is this "taking over" which demonstrates real understanding on the part of the tutee. When the light bulb goes on over the tutee's head, it's very important to give the tutee free reign to explain what he understands and to recognize his own misunderstandings or to identify gaps in what he's learning. Exercise 4-2 focuses on just this issue.

Cultural differences. Cultural differences may lead to misunderstandings as some students will not interrupt and take over an explanation. These students may not have experience in "taking over" or may value politeness to the point that they may indicate understanding when, in fact, they still don't understand. Some students, for example, may consider it impolite to indicate that they didn't understand. Not understanding, in this case, is perceived as insulting the tutor!

Cultures in which males dominate may also influence the success of EALP. Male tutees from such a culture may more frequently interrupt a female tutor. On the other hand, you might expect to see more passivity among female tutees from such a culture, especially if you are a male tutor. In each of these cases, you may find it helpful to exchange views with your tutees about your expectations for tutoring in order to agree about how to proceed.

Before we close this chapter, let's return to the role play exercise with which we began. If what has been covered in this chapter is of value, you should have a more developed set of tools to deal with this problem.

"Promoting Randall's explanation encourages independence"

"Interrupting Randall's explanation discourages independence"

EXERCISE: 4-3

Let's return to the role play situation with which you began this chapter. You may wish to have a different partner. This time, when you play the tutor role, utilize what you've learned throughout this chapter to help you. One of you will act as a tutor, the other as a tutee. The tutor picks the subject matter and begins the session. The tutee's assignment in this role play is to continually attempt to get the tutor to do the explaining. The tutor, of course, must try to provide opportunities for the tutee to do the explaining. Limit your role play to 5 minutes. After the role play, talk about strategies the tutee used to get the tutor to do the explaining. Also, identify ways the tutor attempted to counter the tutee's efforts. Reverse roles and repeat the role play. After both role play episodes have been completed, list strategies actually used; tutee strategies on the left and tutor counter-strategies on the right.

Tutee strategies	Tutor counter-strategies

To what degree did you use what you learned in this chapter?

CONCLUSION

In this chapter, you have learned about two tutoring patterns. Information presented to you was derived from current, state-of-the-art research. The first pattern, Initiation-Reply, is made up of initiations and replies in which either the tutor or the tutee may be the initiator. The initial pattern was also sometimes made up of recurring cycles of initiations and replies: e. g., initiation-reply-initiation-reply.

At a minimum, interaction in IRP identifies the task and checks tutee knowledge. A series of tutor-tutee reply exchanges indicated that the tutor was leading the tutee to an understanding by guided questioning. Tutors utilized initiations such as, "What does this look like?" or "Tell me more about this," or "How would you go about solving that problem?"

Tutees utilized initiations that asked for help or information: "I don't know how to do this type of problem," or "How do I know when a topic sentence is right?"

The Explain-Active Listening Pattern, comprised of explanation and active listening options, offers you and your tutees a way to continue to relate with each other and to continue progressing toward an answer to the existing problem when initiating and replying have not worked. The tutee can explain information to the tutor, provide background, new information, examples, analogies, and so forth. In turn, the tutor can lead the tutee closer to the answer without giving it away by providing some clues about the content or some background information. While one explains (uses explanations), the other either helps the explanation through explanations or supports it through active listening. EALP, then, moves the session forward when IRP breaks down. Tutors tend to move away from initiating and replying before relationship problems or awkwardness becomes an issue. As a result, a regular part of the teaching and learning in tutorials involves sharing information.

IRP and EALP shape the learning encounter between you and your tutees. These patterns facilitate good decisions and flexible thinking in your tutoring. Through these patterns, therefore, your academic knowledge, social skills, and experience can be synthesized into satisfying and beneficial tutoring experiences.

Those needing tutors are often high-risk students, at the greatest risk of dropping out or failing. Therefore, the quality of your decisions and the ease with which you flexibly respond to your individual tutees is very important. Further, many of these high-risk students have in the past been poorly served by their schools. Responding smoothly and sensitively to your students with these patterns may help ensure that past educational inequities do not recur in tutoring programs. The final chapter of this text goes into some depth about tutoring inter-culturally, and thus further enhances your ability to respond well to each of your tutees.

CHAPTER 5: TUTORING IN AN INTER-CULTURAL FRAMEWORK

TUTORING
ROLE

TUTORING
CYCLE

TUTORING
OPTIONS

TUTORING
PATTERNS:

**TUTORING
INTER-
CULTURALLY**

Chapter 5: Tutoring In An Inter-cultural Framework

INTRODUCTION

Tutoring programs are a bright light in education as they bridge gaps between school expectations and students struggling to succeed. Successful tutors and their trainers realize *that many assumptions they initially held about what a good tutee looks like, acts like, learns like, talks like, and so forth may well be invalid.* Cultural differences are vital to explore. Differences in the ways we live, the values we hold, and the customs we are taught are critical to the tutorial process. Once again, you will find yourself in a position to learn as well as teach.

You are part of a very important effort to provide educational opportunity to all students who can succeed. Tutoring, done well, holds great promise. However, having carefully observed and studied hundreds of tutoring sessions and having talked to thousands of tutors and tutees, I have seen potentially positive tutoring relationships between tutors and tutees of different backgrounds become seriously strained or destroyed. Tutoring relationships deteriorate or fall apart despite the efforts of both tutors and tutees to maintain and improve them. Why does this happen and how can it be avoided?

There are no simple answers or formulas which will resolve these questions for you. It is truly a journey you must enter into for which there is no end. I know talking about journeys and the like sounds new age and inexact and so forth. But think about any complex learning you are gaining about human dynamics. Are there any formulas? How do you get along with others? Meet friends? Deal with difficult people and difficult situations? If there were simple methods, these questions would not be so prevalent now and throughout history.

In this text, I can provide you with some important background information and identify characteristics of capable inter-cultural communicators, but it is not possible to tell you to do X or Y and have it really be valuable. Instead, you need experience, thoughtfullness, and information. I can help you organize your thinking and get you started.

The relationships between culture and communication will be explored. The terms communication, culture, inter-cultural communication and inter-cultural framework will be defined. Then eight steps to effective inter-cultural communication will be introduced and explained. There will be Sample Dialogs, Tutoring Situations and Learning Exercises to illustrate and reinforce the content. The overall intent is to help you along in your journey toward an inter-cultural perspective for your tutoring. This will help you to see beyond your perspective and understand the dynamics of the tutoring relationship from the perspective of others.

Superficial generalizations about the characteristics of various cultural groups are simply not useful in developing this expanded perspective. There are simply too many cultures with multiple layers of traditions, experiences, and ways of life to describe in a short text such as this. Brief descriptions of cultural groups run the risk of reducing richly complex and wide-ranging lives of people into a few overdrawn and falsely simplistic statements. This is a misleading approach and can create more of a disservice than a service to both tutors and perceived members of the groups themselves.

COMMUNICATION AND CULTURE

COMMUNICATION

Communication occurs because humans are social: we desire to interact with others. **Communication occurs whenever we do something (e.g., talk, wave, smile) that is observed and responded to by another.** What we communicate includes messages we *intentionally* send (a letter to a friend, saying "hi" to someone in the hallway of your school) and those we *unintentionally* send (slouching, tugging an earlobe, fidgeting, blushing, Freudian slips).

It's important for you to recognize that you communicate with your tutees whether you know it or not because all your messages influence your relationships with your tutees. If, for example, you unintentionally lean away from Judith every time you talk to her, then she might feel you don't like tutoring her.

Your intentions and your actions aren't always in perfect alignment. There are messages you don't want to send, messages you don't intend to send, but you send anyway. Have you ever tried to stop blushing, for example? Been so embarrassed that you couldn't look up? Found yourself talking and couldn't believe what you were saying? 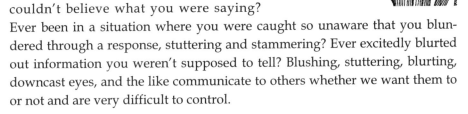 Ever been in a situation where you were caught so unaware that you blundered through a response, stuttering and stammering? Ever excitedly blurted out information you weren't supposed to tell? Blushing, stuttering, blurting, downcast eyes, and the like communicate to others whether we want them to or not and are very difficult to control.

EXERCISE: 5-1

Briefly recount a situation in which you sent a message you didn't intend to send, but sent anyway. Maybe it happened on a date, in a classroom, with other friends, but the key is you clearly sent a message that others received even though you didn't intend it.

_____

_____

_____

_____

_____

We can't not communicate: we can't not interpret. So whether we intend to or not, whether we are aware of it or not, we are always communicating. This is the basis for the phrase you may have heard: **we can't not communicate. Once you let go of the notion that all of our communication is intentional and conscious, then you can see that all of our behaviors around others are messages.** We are always communicating whether we intend to or not, whether we are aware of it or not.

A corollary is that **we are always interpreting messages**. Whether we intend to or not, whether we are aware of it or not, we interpret others' behaviors constantly. What you choose to focus on and how you interpret it is part of your cultural framework.

EXERCISE: 5-2

Arrange to view a videotape of a tutoring session. Identify a behavior by the tutor you think the tutor is unaware of. What message did this behavior send in this situation? (Examples include repeatedly looking at the clock suggesting boredom or anxiety, rapidly tapping the pencil on the table suggesting impatience, and placing a hand over one's mouth suggesting hesitancy to talk.)

behavior _____

message _____

_____

EXERCISE: 5-3

Review the videotape you examined for Exercise 5-2. Look especially for messages which the tutee sent which you think the tutor either didn't perceive or misinterpreted. Identify one missed or misinterpreted message. 1. Describe the message as objectively as you can. In other words, how was the message sent? 2. What do you think was the intent of the message? 3. What did the tutor take the message to mean? In other words, how was it misinterpreted?

description _____

intent _____

misinterpretation _____

CONTEXTUAL: QUALITY OF COMMUNICATIONS

Most importantly, communication is contextual. Contextual means that all communication occurs in some situation. Any situation is a complex set of interacting influences. We are always in some physical environment: a classroom, a library, a city bus on a rain-slickened street in the dead of night, in the middle of a loud rap music concert, and so forth.

At the same time we are always in some social context. Whether we are astronauts in outer space, spectators at a baseball game, or meeting with a college president, we are in some type of situation for which there is "normal" behavior. Baseball fans yell at umpires. Astronauts utilize more clipped formal speech: "Mission Control, that's affirmative." When meeting with the college president, we use more formal forms of address, ("Yes, Dr. Klinkenmeister, I was swinging from the fire escape of the men's dorm, singing 'Girls Just Want To Have Fun,' but . . ."). In a public library or in a museum, we're expected to speak in hushed tones, not yell "Boo" at the librarian or caretaker. Shouting, laughing, put-downs are an expected part of a pick up basketball game among friends, but if you are facing a judge in court for a series of traffic violations, then wearing an old t-shirt and raggedy jeans, calling the arresting officer a "pig," referring to the judge as "Dude," and interrupting the judge while he is speaking could seriously influence the judge's decision about your punishment.

Your tutoring occurs in a physical and social context which influences communication. For example, if all your tables are round, then you and

Notes:

your tutees will be partly facing each other. If the environment is very quiet, then you will likely speak softly, and so forth. Socially, tutors are expected to be respectful to program staff, to other tutors, and to students. Ironically, we rarely talk about these rules except to admonish those who break them. We are all expected to know and follow them.

EXERCISE: 5-4

In your opinion, how are tutors and tutees expected to behave in the area where your tutoring occurs? Write your responses as expectations. The first one is written for you.

1. <u>Tutees are expected to arrive for tutoring on time.</u>

2. _____

3. _____

4. _____

5. _____

CULTURE

Tutoring, like all communication, is a complex, intricate collection of messages and responses occurring in a social and physical context. In a broad sense, the complete social environment in which you grew up and of which you are now a part constitutes your culture. **Your culture consists of a set of socially transmitted behavior patterns, beliefs, values, creative works and processes, institutions, and so forth**. Cultures can be distinguished on the basis of race: Asian, Hispanic, Black, Native American. Cultures can be distinguished by nationality: Cambodians, Nicaraguans, Ukrainians, Lebanese, Germans, Eritreans, and so forth. Cultures can be distinguished by socio-economic status: impoverished homeless, privileged wealthy living on huge estates, middle-class farmer on a family farm. Cultures can be distinguished by language: dozens of languages are spoken in most big cities. Because all humans are members of at least one culture, all human communication occurs in the context of at least one culture, and possibly more.

Within the United States, increasing numbers of people from hundreds of cultures are redefining what American culture means. Immigration patterns have shifted, influencing life in the U.S. with various cultures from Southeast Asia, Central and South America, the Middle East, and so forth. Technological advances in media and in transportation put people from different parts of the world in contact with each other. These changes are apparent in our city streets, in our marketplaces, and, most importantly for you, in our schools. Represented within your group of tutors are likely several different cultures. Represented within your group of tutees are likely even more cultures. Further, represented in any individual are a whole set of cultural influences, especially as we recall that culture is a part not just of race, but can be gender, age, geography, even academic discipline.

Notes:

EXERCISE: 5-5

Complete the following charts. Consult with your tutor trainer about where to secure this information. In the first chart, indicate the percentage of tutors, tutees, and all students by race for each heading. You may wish to alter the categories according to how your school gathers records. Remember that race is only one of many ways to identify cultural differences. In the second chart, indicate the percentage of students by sex.

Culture by Race	Tutors	Tutees	All Students
Asian	_____%	_____%	_____%
Black	_____%	_____%	_____%
Hispanic	_____%	_____%	_____%
Native American	_____%	_____%	_____%
White	_____%	_____%	_____%
Culture by Sex	Tutors	Tutees	All Students
Female	_____%	_____%	_____%
Male	_____%	_____%	_____%

INTER-CULTURAL TUTORING

Regardless of your own background or the school you work for, you are likely, possibly certain, to be working with students from cultures different than yours. When tutoring occurs between a tutor and a tutee who are not of the same culture, it is called **inter-cultural tutoring**.

Inter-cultural tutoring, like all inter-cultural communication, is loaded with opportunities for new learning and experiences, filled with the potential excitement of discovering similarities and celebrating differences, and the reawakening of respect for the diverse manifestations of human experience among our brothers and sisters from all over the world. At the same time, inter-cultural tutoring is loaded with opportunities for misunderstanding and criticism, for feelings of isolation, hurt, and resentment. Old wounds unrelated to your tutoring, but painful nonetheless, can be reopened and exacerbated. New wounds can be inflicted.

I think I know the question on your mind right now: How can I engage most effectively in inter-cultural communication?

EFFECTIVE INTER-CULTURAL COMMUNICATION

Communication is effective when people understand the relationship between culture and communication. As discussed earlier, **culture is the framework any individual brings to any communication**. Everything any individual initially knows about how to communicate comes from one's culture. We learn how to communicate and how to interpret the things that are said to us. Different people learn this in different ways. As a result, *we don't learn ways of identifying and allowing for these differences.* So we have "our way of communicating" and no way of communicating effectively with people with different "ways of communicating."

Example #1. I can recall traveling in Mexico and hearing another American tourist say, obviously frustrated at not being understood by a Mexican shopkeeper, "Can't these people speak English?" Well, many can, but our frustrated traveler is in Mexico, where the first language of more than 90% of the population is Spanish. He was not accounting for his learned cultural framework: that all effective communication occurs in a language familiar to *him*.

Example #2. In the same vein, a frustrated tutor once lamented that her tutee, born and raised in Laos, Southeast Asia, "just couldn't get verb tenses." Our frustrated tutor said, "She must have a mental block. It's gotta be like verb tenses in her Laotian language only with English words!" The

Communication is effective when people understand the relationship between culture and communication.

tutor's assumption that all languages have verb tenses like English didn't account for the fact that different languages may be structured in markedly different ways. The tutor's unquestioned cultural framework dictated that languages of any type utilize verb tenses just like English. The tutor is unaware that generally, all Southeast Asian languages utilize information included in the talk, not derivations of verbs, to help a listener identify time frames. Changes in verb endings or in helping verbs were not a part of the tutee's experiences, but they are an integral part of the tutor's experiences. Certainly the tutee needs to master verb tenses to achieve fluency in English. Assumptions can be dangerous in tutoring. A tutor who does not question cultural frameworks can find learning and the tutorial relationship severely impeded.

CULTURE AS A FRAMEWORK

The most important thing you need to know to tutor effectively is that the mental framework (cultural experiences and learning) you use in school or in tutoring may be quite different from that of each of your tutees. For both you and your tutees, this cultural framework influences all communication with others. This means that both message *sending* and message *interpreting* are controlled by your framework. Further, this framework — or at least many parts of it — is so ingrained in each of us that we aren't aware of it, except in the most general way. So we often make judgements about people based on our frameworks without being aware of it.

A INTER-CULTURAL FRAMEWORK

Your goal, then, for your tutoring, is to develop **an inter-cultural framework**. If you understand that there are differences and if you can account for the different frameworks and experiences of yourself and your tutees, then your tutoring can help all of your students become more effective, efficient, and confident learners. You can successfully fulfill the Tutoring Mission and Goals (Chapter 1), understand and utilize the steps in the Tutoring Cycle (Chapter 2), and master the Options for Tutoring Talk (Chapter 3).

Figure 1 represents a inter-cultural framework for tutoring. The rectangle encompassing both you and the tutee depicts this larger framework. Having a broader framework allows you to step out of the situation and analyze what's happening as though you were an observer. Observing while you are participating may sound impossible. How can I be in it and be outside looking at it at the same time? Humans are capable of occupying both positions simultaneously; this ability is in fact standard equipment on all humans. You will always be a product of your culture, but you can develop the ability to understand inter-cultural tutoring from a broader perspective. This broader perspective gives you *an inter-cultural framework for your tutoring*.

Notes:

Figure 5-1 - An inter-cultural framework for master tutoring

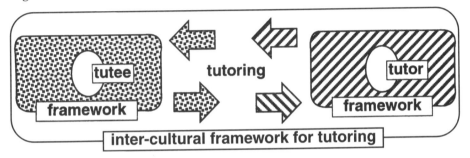

COMPONENTS OF AN INTER-CULTURAL FRAMEWORK

Introduced in the following list are eight components of an inter-cultural framework. Developing your skills as an effective inter-cultural tutor involves continually developing your understanding of each of these components and your understanding of how they connect to each other. As you read through these, think about how they apply to you and the individuals you tutor.

1. Commitment

One simple but essential component to effective inter-cultural tutoring is your commitment to your tutees. If you truly desire to communicate effectively and to enter into a mutually respectful relationship, then your effectiveness will be drastically enhanced. Ever been in a situation where your teacher seemed to be just going through the motions? I know I have.

My long-time friend and I still remember Mr. King, our eleventh grade history teacher, for his apparent lack of commitment. To the best of our memory all he ever did in class was read to us from the assigned chapter in the history book. He

COMPONENTS OF INTER-CULTURAL FRAMEWORK

1. Commitment
2. Acceptance
3. Empathy
4. Filtered Perception
5. Us and Them
6. Discrimination Institutionalized
7. Generalize Cautiously
8. Solicit, Accept, and Reflect on Feedback

Notes:

would start immediately after taking role. He didn't embellish or emphasize or explain; he merely read verbatim, head bowed. When the bell rang, he stopped. In the next class period he would pick up where he left off the day before. He hadn't made a commitment to be a good teacher. We students in the class had almost no relationship with him and little involvement with learning. We felt class to be a waste of time. Because we felt he didn't care about us or about the subject, we gave significantly less than our best effort.

<u>Implications for tutoring</u>. The same is true for your tutoring. Giving your best effort in each session requires your commitment to making tutoring work and to developing a productive relationship with each tutee. If you are committed to this, then you have the best chance of making it work.

<u>2. Acceptance</u>

Acceptance in this context means to be receptive to others and their experiences. Although you may be culturally different from some or many of your tutees, acceptance means to enjoy the differences by not judging them and to accept the meaning people apply to their experiences. This kind of acceptance is akin to listening carefully as discussed in Chapter 2. If you really listen to others, you can begin to understand their worlds and how they each make sense of their world.

<u>Implications for tutoring</u>. The point of acceptance is to first be aware that there are differences between people of different cultures which can be found in all facets of their daily lives. Second, please recognize that these differences can't be grouped into better or worse because the very act of grouping brings values into play, and by definition values are culturally transmitted. Not judging one way as better or worse than another equals acceptance.

> **COMPONENTS OF INTER-CULTURAL FRAMEWORK**
>
> 1. Commitment
> 2. Acceptance
> 3. Empathy
> 4. Filtered Perception
> 5. Us and Them
> 6. Discrimination Institutionalized
> 7. Generalize Cautiously
> 8. Solicit, Accept, and Reflect on Feedback

<u>3. Empathy</u>

Empathy means understanding another's feelings from within that person's framework. What does it feel like to be your tutees? How does each of them experience the world?

EXERCISE: 5-6

Think of all the tutees you have worked with recently. With which tutee did you have the most difficulty? Imagine yourself to be this tutee. As best you can and completely from the tutee's perspective, describe his/her perceptions of you and the tutoring s/he received. What did this tutee see, hear, think, and feel during your tutoring? Try to write it in his/her voice: that is, write it in words and phrases you think s/he would use. After you finish, review what you have written. What did you learn about yourself by seeing yourself through your tutee's eyes?

_____

_____

_____

_____

_____

EXERCISE: 5-7

List your three best friends in the space below. List the ones you genuinely "hang out with" the most. Note their race, first language, and age. To what degree are your best friends different from you? To what degree are they similar? Most of you will find that your friends are quite similar to you. My purpose is not to criticize anyone for this similarity, but to indicate that we tend to have the most in-depth experiences with similar people.

	first name	race	1st language	age
friend #1:				
friend #2				
friend #3				

4. Filtered Perception

Perception is the subjective interpretation of selected external stimuli. No one perceives everything, and no one perceives things without interpretation. It may surprise you that part of what we learn as we grow up in our culture is how and what to perceive. Our senses of touch, taste, sight, sound, and smell are not open pipelines between us and the outside world. Instead, our perceptions are learned and thus both imperfectly filtered and unconsciously interpreted. Assuming Mom cooks, what does Mom's home cooking smell like? Does it smell like Southern fried chicken, rich tomato sauce, Christmas tamales, or steamed rice and salted fish? If you are Burmese, you may smell sharp garlic, hot chiles, lemongrass, and coconut milk. Whatever Mom's home cooking smells like to you, you have learned it. *From our cultural experiences and training, we learn to "tune out" some stimuli and to pay close attention to other stimuli.*

Perception is a series of filters through which we see and hear only what we learn to see and hear. Our brains save us from sensory overload by eliminating much of what we might perceive and attending closely to other stimuli. From our cultural experiences we learn what to attend to and what to filter out.

<u>Language</u>. You can certainly see selective perception operating in language. If, for example, English is your only language until you begin to learn Spanish in college, you initially may not notice that the Spanish sound assigned to the letter "b" is pronounced somewhere between the English pronunciations of "b" and "v." If you are Spanish learning English, you may not notice a difference between the English "b" and "v" sounds.

Another difference is in the assignment of a masculine or feminine quality to nouns. In Spanish and other Romance languages, all nouns are either masculine or feminine. In English they are not.

Voice inflection is another important factor in determining meaning in some languages and less so in others. If you are learning Thai, for example, you may not notice that words given the same letter sounds are given different meanings according to intonation. Thai intonations include a rising sound, a falling sound, a flat sound, a rising-falling combination, and a falling-rising combination. The Thai word "mai" for example takes on a different meaning with each different intonation.

Given the nature of the language we learn as children, we learn to be sensitive to different features of language. So Thai children learn to be very attentive to inflections and Latin American children learn whether objects are masculine or feminine. English-speaking children learn the importance of time in part because of the attention to time frames via verb tenses. To be an accepted member of one's culture, one must learn to perceive the same things in the same ways as other members.

Our cultural learning also teaches us to assign meaning to what we perceive. If you saw a man place his hand gently on the head of a child, you would likely "see" an affectionate gesture. After all, in the U. S. most people know that one way to show affection to a youngster is by tousling hair or stroking a head. In this case, we interpret what we see. What you see is the hand gently on the head. The interpretation involves assigning the *meaning* of affection to the *gesture* of head touching. Were a Thai person to observe the same behavior, he or she would "see" profound disrespect. To Thais, the head is the highest part of the body (physically and spiritually) and so should not be touched by others.

<u>Implications for tutoring</u>. For you as tutor, the implications of the nature of perception are profound. What you see and the meaning you assign what you see are automatic, but not always accurate or appropriate. That which you have learned to perceive influences your judgments.

For example, in what is popularly termed "Black English," the word "be" is used as a helping verb, as in "I be going home now." Many non-Blacks ascribe ignorance and lack of grammatical form to this type of statement. In fact, as linguists such as William LaBov have demonstrated, the use of "be" as a helping verb is consistently used and understood by Black English speakers according to a set of followable rules. In other words, within the cultural context of Black English speakers, the use of "be" as a helping verb is appropriate and proper. Further, speakers are consistent in how it is used. If you are a tutor familiar with Black English, then you can develop a much stronger bond with a non-Black English speaking tutee if you recognize and respect the differences between your version of English and the tutee's version of English. The reverse is also true. If your tutee utilizes Black English and you don't, recognizing and respecting differences will enhance your tutoring relationship. *The fact that each of the languages differs somewhat from the other doesn't reduce the validity of either in the context for which it is useful.*

Notes:

What you see and the meaning you assign what you see are automatic, but not always accurate or appropriate.

Notes: ✍

The core of this situation is that Burnett's learned language system is at odds with the expectations of Dr. D'Etat. Burnett needs to understand that this is the issue and to make an informed decision as to what to do about it. Felicia's best strategy is to remain in the facilitator role, help Burnett devise and follow through on steps to take to resolve the situation. The steps are likely to be: (1) understand the situation; (2) identify options; (3) discuss options with informed sources such as Dr. D'Etat, a trusted English teacher, a counselor, other students, or yourself; and (4) select an option and devise a plan. Felicia can help Burnett but she can't decide for him. He may decide his best option is to drop the class and take it next semester from someone else. He may decide to stay in the class and meet regularly with a writing tutor for help with his essays. Or he may select some other course of action. The key is that what to do is Burnett's decision. Felicia's role is to help him learn how to prepare to make that decision.

The example of "be" in Black English is just one of hundreds of potential instances where differences occur between you and your tutees. In each case, you will be selectively perceiving, reducing the flow of understanding, through the communication channel between you. In general, tutors who are white and middle class need to be particularly aware of the influence of perception on tutoring. This is not because white middle class tutors are less able, more biased, or any of the rest of that stuff.

<u>Experience with two cultures</u>. It is because compared to many Asian Americans, African Americans, Hispanic Americans, and Native Americans, white middle-class tutors are less likely to be experienced with coping with two cultural worlds. An Asian American person, for example, may have learned in childhood how to function well in an Asian American context, at family get togethers, at religious services, cultural holidays and so forth. At the same time, by virtue of being a minority in a larger culture, that same Asian American student will have had to learn to deal with the middle-class white culture because it is dominant in United States' society. One likely encounters it in classrooms, at the mall, at the auto repair shop, at the motor vehicle department and so forth.

From these encounters, one who is not of the dominant majority necessarily learns how to function with people who are. After all, a majority means that there are more of them and so a minority is more likely to encounter them. Generally, those people most like the dominant culture experience the least social pressure to learn how to function within the context of a different culture.

5. Us and Them

Every group by definition is an "us," and everyone not in the group belongs to "them." "Us and them" thinking is so built into our everyday interaction that we don't recognize it. Unconscious notions of who is in the "us group" and who is in the "them group" are played out subtly but powerfully in moment to moment talk in all social and work groups.

Remember the concept "The China Syndrome," dramatized in a movie of the same name? The China Syndrome refers to the theoretical possibility that an accidental overheating of a nuclear reactor core could lead to the contents melting through the storage container, eating through the earth below, and burning all the way through the earth to emerge at the other side. The "other side" is China. Think about the name for this concept. From which side of the earth do people who coined the term "China Syndrome" come from? People in China are "them."

Is there a community near you labeled "Chinatown?" Who do you suppose gave it the name? The very name "Chinatown" reveals that it is distinguished by the fact that its inhabitants are a "them:" in this case Chinese. Does anybody call some other part of town Whiteytown? If there is an area called Whiteytown in a city near you (which I really doubt), why does it never show up on AAA maps? Chinatown does. In New York City, for example, there is a Chinatown, a Little Italy, a Greektown, and so forth. But there is no Anglotown.

I'm not entering into a discussion of whether there should be names like Chinatown, but rather using it to illustrate the point that what distinguished a certain portion of the city is that Chinese people live in it and that therefore, this section of the city is "different." By implication, there is an "our section of the city" which is not different because it is us. For many, the inner city is where "they" live. For others, the inner city is where "we" live.

"Us and them thinking" in schools. In schools, "us" and "them" thinking also exists in subtle but powerful ways. Researchers have chronicled examples such as the following. In a U. S. History class, many teachers explain the Manhattan Purchase to classes which include Native Americans in the following way: "We bought Manhattan from the Indians for less than $30 in beads and trinkets." The use of the term "we" subtly tells Native Americans that they are a "them" and subtly tells non-Native Americans that they are an "us." Being one of us signals preferred status within a group. Further, this story is told from the point of view of the purchasers, not the sellers.

A similar message goes to African Americans when a teacher or a tutor says that "Lincoln freed *them*." When we assume doctors are male or that nurses are female, a similar message is sent to women. When a collection of works labeled "great books" are all authored by Western European males, only Western European males are in the "we" group. In the individual case, these examples seem insignificant. When aggregated over a class hour, a school day, an academic year, and a school career, they are a very powerful but unacknowledged part of the school curriculum which subtly divides students into us and them categories by race, by gender, or by some other feature.

Notes:

This combination of messages leads to what sociologists and social psychologists call **"otherness." Otherness is defined as a culturally learned awareness that one is not included in the mainstream of a society and that one is different from those who are in the mainstream**. In his autobiography, Malcolm X experienced otherness when he was a young student getting the best grades in his class and his teacher specifically told him he could not be a lawyer because of his race.

My wife is an architect. Early in her career before I met her, she experienced otherness when a co-worker admonished her for holding a position in a prestigious architectural firm which he thought should go to a man. "After all," he explained, "a man has a family to support." My wife was a single parent at that time. A number of news shows emphasizing investigative journalism (e.g., "60 Minutes" and "Frontline") have documented differential treatment of individuals according to race in such areas as housing, jobs, retail purchasing, and social acceptance.

<u>Implications for tutoring</u>. The experiences of those traditionally not in the majority culture are more likely to include discrimination and exclusion. By being sensitive to this, you can better enter into and develop productive working relationships with tutees. You have been selected to be a tutor partly because you have good interpersonal skills. Incorporate what you learn here into your already considerable skills. Don't waste time feeling guilty or taking responsibility for actions of others.

EXERCISE: 5-9

Make a list of your interpersonal skills. What do you think you do well that helps you relate to people? Are you a good listener? Are you quick to sense other's moods and feelings? Are you friendly? Articulate? Open? Try to overcome training many of us experience which says that it is egotistical and offensive to say good things about oneself.

_____

_____

_____

TUTORING INTER-CULTURALLY

Notes:

6. Discrimination Institutionalized

Many students have not been served well by their schools and, as a result, they may approach you with some degree of skepticism. In a society in which we espouse values of inclusion of all, opportunity for all, and fair-treatment to all, those who seem "different" are often systematically excluded, denied opportunities, and treated unfairly. The following two of innumerable examples demonstrate. Both of these examples are taken from public records regarding well-documented cases. Even a casual researcher could find many other current examples from court decisions, newspapers, and news magazines.

Rockford, Illinois. In this mid-size manufacturing city, a court recently found that students were separated and treated differently by race, not need or ability, according to a syndicated article in the Los Angeles Times newspaper appearing in early November of 1993. Despite an earlier court ruling requiring the district to desegregate, systematic and flagrant inequities kept students socially and academically segregated. The abuses took many forms. For example, after arriving at school in the morning, Latino students were forced to wait on the bus which brought them until classes began. At the same time, white students had full use of the playground and equipment. At many schools in the district, black and white children ate at separate lunch times, entered through separate doors, and used separate bathrooms in separate corridors.

Academic segregation was equally horrific. Beginning in kindergarten, all white students were tracked into honors and college prep classes, but minorities, including those scoring at the 99th percentile in testing, were routinely consigned to slow-learner sections. Once assigned a track, it was nearly impossible to be assigned to another.

The judge in the case has written that the school district committed "such open acts of discrimination as to be cruel," and committed other acts "with such subtlety as to raise discrimination to an art form." Ironically, school administrators, those with responsibility for the quality of education offered to students, confirmed the judge's assessment. The superintendent of the district, for example, acknowledged the truth of the allegations and cited reasons for the district's isolating tactics: pressure from white parents, incompetence, and officials who didn't realize the effects. "No reason is defensible," he admitted. Another district official, concerned for his job and so remaining anonymous, called district tracking "a system of apartheid."

You may have experienced this type of discrimination in your own school career and so you know the hurt, distrust, and anger which can result from such fundamental and overwhelming injustice. If you haven't experienced this kind of discrimination, imagine how you would feel if the society around you continually directed it toward you and felt justified in doing so.

110   TUTORING INTER-CULTURALLY

<u>Central Valley area, California.</u> An extensive federal lawsuit resulted in a ruling against a medium-sized city in the state's farming region for flagrant abuses of power in drawing school district boundaries and providing school funding. District boundary lines literally went down some city streets, circling some houses to include the residents and going around other houses to exclude specific others. The courts found that the lines were shown to provide favorable schools to children in the included houses, many of them belonging to city officials, and less favorable schools to children of other residents, many of whom were African American or Hispanic American. Further, schools attended by children of city fathers received higher levels of funding. Scholar John Ogbu at the University of California has written extensively about this case.

Tragically, providing genuine opportunities for educational success to all of our citizens is constantly imperiled and too often a sham. Inequities are unfortunately built into our society and so inherently are a part of any aspect of society, including schools, unless we act to make change. In the schools, it means that many students who are perceived by those in control as "different" don't have the same chance as students not perceived as different.

<u>Implications for tutoring</u>. One important consequence for you as a tutor is that your tutees may not have the same faith in schools as you do. The reverse may also be true. If you survived inequities such as those described above, you may be much more cynical about school than some of your tutees. Either way, it is important to understand that we all have different attitudes toward school, depending in large part on our experiences. If you are fair, communicate clearly, and are open to people different than you, then your relationships with each tutee can be mutually positive and productive.

7. Generalize Cautiously

You may be a minority tutor who experienced little discrimination in schools. Conversely, you may work with a white student who did experience some kind of discrimination in schools. You can't assume that every white person had every advantage in school and that every African American student had every disadvantage. Is every white person an oppressor? Is every black person automatically disenfranchised from society? Do all dark skinned people speak or understand Black English? Does everyone with a last name of Garcia speak Spanish first and English second? Obviously not. Not any more than every woman is a good cook, every guy understands machinery and knows directions to obscure locations, every older person is wise (take me for example), every teacher caring, every person who drinks alcohol addicted and abusive, and so forth.

If you are fair, communicate clearly, and are open to people different than you, then your relationships with each tutee can be mutually positive and productive.

Generalizations about a group don't necessarily apply to a given individual in that group. While many U. S. citizens with the last name Garcia do speak Spanish, it would be foolish to assume that a certain individual named Garcia therefore speaks Spanish. Some men are excellent cooks and do much of the cooking for their families.

Stereotyping. A related kind of quick generalizing, but which is not based on any group reality is **stereotyping: the erroneous assignment of characteristics or qualities to people because of some set of superficial features**. We're all familiar with stereotypes. Lawyers are greedy, conscience-less egomaniacs. This stereotype is so prevalent that a popular beer advertisement features lawyer roping. Many laugh at this "joke" because it *seems* true. That is, it fits the stereotype. Women in short skirts are "asking for it." Blacks are lazy. Irish are drunks. White males in cowboy boots and hats are intolerant. Teachers teach because they can't do what they teach. Etc., etc., etc.

EXERCISE: 5-10

Recently, while waiting at the checkout line at the grocery store, a white woman behind me whispered a derogatory comment about the black woman in line ahead of us. The woman behind me first pointed out steaks, a cake from the store bakery, and a $12 bottle of wine among the items in the Black woman's basket. The woman behind me then whispered, "Food Stamps. Look at that. You and me paid for those steaks and the rest of that stuff." The complainer behind me literally did not perceive that the woman in front of us paid for all her groceries with a personal check. No food stamps were discussed or in evidence. In the mind of the complainer behind me, a stereotype was applied and confirmed. In the space below, identify the stereotypes which seemed to be in the mind of the complaining shopper behind me. Explain how the stereotypes influenced her perceptions.

_____

_____

_____

_____

_____

Despite their obvious and gross distortions, one insidious quality of stereotypes is that they are self-confirming. Because we see what we learn to see, we tend to interpret behavior according to learned stereotypes, further reinforcing the stereotype. We also tend to see only information which confirms stereotypes and not remember information which is contradictory.

<u>Implications for tutoring</u>. While it is true that we are members of groups, we are also distinct individuals. Few if any groups are made up of people formed from the same batch of dough and cut by the same cookie cutter. In your tutoring, utilize what you know about groups of people cautiously. Focus on the individuals you work with, utilizing what you know about their backgrounds as *possible* influences. Be aware of stereotypes in your own thinking.

8. Solicit, Accept, and Reflect on Feedback

There's no way this guidebook or any other training can fully prepare you beforehand to be a perfect communicator with any person you meet. Just as you learn to swim by getting in the pool, to drive by getting behind the wheel of a car, to be intimate by . . . (well, skip that one), you learn to tutor from a inter-cultural framework by interacting with others.

As a previous exercise has already tried to reinforce, you have considerable skills already. Put them to work. You will learn by communicating with others and by listening to others. Don't be afraid to talk about communication with those with whom you communicate. You'll find in most cases that talking about what's happening has a tremendous potential to ease tension and create the bonds of understanding.

Don't be afraid to talk about communication with those with whom you communicate . . . . . talking has a tremendous potential to ease tension and create the bonds of understanding.

Much research has shown that more effective teachers reflect on their teaching. They think about what they are going to do beforehand and analyze how it went afterward. The purpose of these eight components of effective inter-cultural tutoring is to give you some guidance as to how to prepare for your tutoring and how to evaluate it afterward. These guidelines have been culled from a great deal of research and reading in communication, culture, and effective tutoring.

You can augment the information contained here by asking others about the various cultures you encounter in your tutoring. Your tutor trainer

Notes:

can guide you to knowledgeable people as well as being a source of informatin for you. College teachers you have come to know can also give you insights and referrals to knowledgeable outhers. Fellow tutors can talk to you about their backgrounds and how it influences their communication with and acceptance by others. As you continue to inform yourself, the process by which you plan your tutoring and evaluate it will become even more sophisticated and so will you. For review, the components of an inter-cultural framework are listed again here.

COMPONENTS OF INTER-CULTURAL FRAMEWORK

1. Commitment
2. Acceptance
3. Empathy
4. Filtered Perception
5. Us and Them
6. Discrimination Institutionalized
7. Generalize Cautiously
8. Solicit, Accept, and Reflect on Feedback

EXERCISE: 5-11

Over the next week, pay attention to your encounters with others of different backgrounds, particularly in your tutoring. Make a point of learning something about a person from a culture different than your own. What you learn can be on any topic: language, the role of women, school practices, religious beliefs or observances, social manners, whatever. If you have no occasion to learn by interacting with a person of another culture, then seek out the assistance of a knowledgeable other. Ask about a culture you have encountered or are likely to encounter in your tutoring. Whatever the source of your information, summarize an interesting or important piece of information below. Remember that one person's perceptions of their own culture are not likely to be universally the same as other members of that same culture.

_____

_____

_____

_____

CONCLUSION

In this chapter, you have learned (a) that what and how we communicate is a product of our respective cultures; (b) that because cultures differ, our communication processes differ; and (c) that therefore, considerable opportunity for misunderstanding and ill-will exists in inter-cultural tutoring. However, (d) developing an inter-cultural framework and utilizing the components of effective inter-cultural tutoring can lead to successful, productive, and enjoyable tutoring relationships with all students whom you tutor. Finally, (e) this process can be further enhanced by your continued learning about and experiences with people from backgrounds different from your own.

CONCLUSION

You have experienced a tutor training program which has been shown to consistently improve the quality of tutoring sessions. Tutor trainers, program directors, and other staff from over 450 colleges have undergone earlier versions of this training in over a dozen workshops at institutes, conferences, and invited sessions. This Guidebook combines extensive research with all those training experiences. The training you will receive with the aid of <u>The Master Tutor</u> is based on the most advanced and reliable knowledge about tutoring that exists.

Notes:

INFORMED DECISIONS

As I said at the beginning, you have become involved in tutoring because of your expertise in a subject area and your abilities to work effectively with people. Your tutoring can be improved with training; you can be more effective if you are better informed. No piece of information or bit of advice, however, is as valuable as your decision-making skills. It is these skills, augmented by some guidance and information from this Guidebook and your other training experiences, which will help you become a MASTER TUTOR.

Therefore, the mission of this Guidebook has been to provide you with appropriate and accurate information which guides your decision making. In addition to helping you make good decisions, I intend to help you be flexible in your approaches to the infinite variety of situations, to encourage you to reflect on and learn from your own tutoring experiences, and to remain respectful of differences between yourself and your tutees.

SUMMARY OF TEXT

In Chapter 1: The Tutoring Role, you learned about the expectations placed on a tutor and about the goals of tutoring. The information in that chapter intended to help you know directions to take and to recognize situations which deviate from that direction. Following these goals defines your role.

In Chapter 2: The Tutoring Cycle, you learned about a basic sequence which, when followed, structures a tutoring encounter and emphasizes student learning as a result of the students' efforts. The Tutoring Cycle is given reality by what you do and how you do it. Of particular importance are the steps which help students learn *how to learn*.

In Chapter 3: Tutoring Options, six choices for your behavior are explained. You or your tutees can initiate, reply, evaluate, explain, use active listening and be quiet. Choosing among options is guided by your goal of

Notes:

providing opportunity. More effective tutors provide the tutee the opportunity to do the work and figure out problems. In many ways, the art of tutoring is in providing just enough influence to get tutees on track and keep them there.

Chapter 4: Tutoring Patterns covers two basic ways tutors and tutees interact. One involves a series of the initiation and reply options in a question-answer format. The other involves combinations of the explain and active listening options. More effective tutors utilize the explain and active listening pattern with the tutee taking the lead in explaining. More effective tutors also avoid giving extensive replies to tutee initiations.

The last chapter, Tutoring In an Inter-cultural Framework, promotes your respect for students of all backgrounds. Each person comes to tutoring with an individual world view. This view is a framework filtering what we perceive and influencing how we communicate.

In sum, being a MASTER TUTOR involves (a) understanding your role, (b) following The Tutoring Cycle, (c) utilizing your options effectively, (d) promoting the tutee's lead in the informational pattern, and (e) developing an inter-cultural framework for your tutoring.

POST-TRAINING ASSESSMENT

Now is the time to complete your final two exercises. These are exact duplicates of the self-assessments you took in the Introduction, providing you the opportunity to gauge for yourself some of the effects of the training you have received. The first exercise assesses your knowledge of tutoring; the second, your skills as a tutor.

EXERCISE: ASSESS YOUR KNOWLEDGE

The following questionnaire tests your understanding of tutoring. Indicate whether each statement is true or false by placing a "T" or an "F" on the line.

____ 1. It's my role to help my students with whatever they need help with. (Ch. 1)

____ 2. If a tutee I work with doesn't get the information, then I am responsible. (Ch. 1)

____ 3. I know that I will encounter some students who have no motivation. (Ch. 1)

____ 4. If I feel that I have been assigned to work with a student whose needs are beyond my ability to help, then I should tell my supervisor right away. (Ch. 1)

____ 5. At the beginning of every tutoring session, the tutor and I should plan the session and set an agenda for it, even if it takes two or three minutes. (Ch. 2)

____ 6. I would expect that in tutoring sessions, tutees should do more explaining than their tutors. (Ch. 3)

____ 7. It's critically important that I praise my tutees liberally. (Ch. 3)

____ 8. Providing clear and accurate explanations to the tutee is at the heart of my best tutoring. (Ch. 3 and 4)

____ 9. Asking good questions is at the heart of my best tutoring. (Ch. 3 and 4)

____ 10. Compared to me, at least some of the students I work with are likely to have very different attitudes toward school and the subjects I tutor. (Ch. 5)

____ 11. It's important for me to trust my perceptions. (Ch. 5)

____ 12. My students must learn standard English and I should teach them. (Ch. 5)

____ TOTAL

Answers on following page

Notes:

So how did you do? Compare your score to your Pre-Test score in the Introduction. Did you improve? If so, Congratulations! If not, go back over those numbered chapters that are listed after each statement.

In this next exercise, you will assess your skills. In this exercise there are no right answers, just your own self-evaluation.

EXERCISE: ASSESS YOUR SKILLS

Rate yourself on each statement. Place the appropriate number on the line at the front of the statement.
1: strongly agree 2: agree 3: neither agree nor disagree
4: disagree 5: strongly disagree

_____ 1. I am committed to being a good tutor.

_____ 2. I am able to objectively evaluate myself.

_____ 3. People would generally say I am a good listener.

_____ 4. I can explain to others how to learn the subjects I tutor.

_____ 5. I am able to explain the same idea in several different ways.

_____ 6. I have a repertoire of skills for communicating effectively with others.

_____ 7. I am open to new ideas and new perspectives.

_____ 8. I have the sensitivity and self-awareness to understand how I am different from each of my tutees.

_____ 9. I am able to adjust my tutoring according to the individual characteristics of my tutees.

_____ 10. At this point I understand how to tutor successfully.

Compare your rating to your Pre-Test rating in the Introduction. Have positive changes occurred? If so, Congratulations!

GOOD-BYE FOR NOW

As I said in the Introduction, I genuinely welcome your comments, suggestions, questions, and interesting experiences about tutoring. You may contact me via the publisher whose address is on an early page of this guide-book or kindly complete and mail the comment letter printed on the next page. I wish you enjoyable, productive tutoring experiences.

Thanks For Your Commitment!
Dr. Ross B. MacDonald

Notes:

Dr. MacDonald
c/o The Cambridge Stratford Study Skills Institute
   8560 Main Street, Williamsville, N.Y. 14221
      e-mail: cambridges@aol.com

Dear Dr. MacDonald:

The things I most liked about <u>The Master Tutor</u> were _____
_____
_____

The things I most disliked were _____
_____
_____

If I were to change, add or delete, I would suggest you _____
_____
_____

My general comments for publication in your next edition are _____
_____
_____

                                        Sincerely,

                                        Signed _____

                                        Name _____

                                        Address _____

                                        _____ Zip _____

                                        Telephone (   ) _____
                                                   AREA CODE

Using the space below or another sheet of paper, please feel free to tell me about unusual or puzzling tutoring experiences. I promise to write back to you promptly with suggestions or comments.

                                        Dr. Ross B. MacDonald

_____
_____
_____

Notes:

Notes:

Notes: ✐

Notes: